Kenneth H. Carter Jr.

Foreword by Stanley Hauerwas
and Will Willimon

D0168071

EMBRACING

the

WIDENESS

The Shared Convictions
of The United Methodist Church

Abingdon Press™
Nashville

EMBRACING THE WIDENESS:
THE SHARED CONVICTIONS OF THE UNITED METHODIST CHURCH

Copyright © 2018 by Abingdon Press

This book is printed on acid-free paper.

Library of Congress Cataloging-in-Publication Data has been requested.

978-1-5018-7156-6

18 19 20 21 22 23 24 25 26 27—10 9 8 7 6 5 4 3 2 1
MANUFACTURED IN THE UNITED STATES OF AMERICA

CONTENTS

Praise for *Embracing the Wideness*

"Whatever else it may be, the polarization that currently afflicts The United Methodist Church is a result of our surrender to the spirit of the world rather than to the Spirit of Christ. In this simple and profound book, Ken Carter makes the case for a generous orthodoxy that has the power to transcend the political and cultural boxes that divide us so profoundly. Carter convincingly demonstrates that generous orthodoxy is not the property of the left or right, of traditionalists or progressives. It is the heart and marrow of a Church that lives from the generosity of the triune God, and so is able to extend the offer of redeeming grace to all."

—R. Kendall Soulen, Professor of Systematic Theology, Candler School of Theology, Emory University, Atlanta, GA

"For a church seeking a way out, a way out of its disciplinary disagreement, and by some, a way out of the denomination, Ken Carter invites us to a way in. *Embracing the Wideness* lays out a way into a deeper relationship with God and one another, a deeper understanding of scriptural covenant and justice to give the church a foundation for a wider unity and expanded mission."

—John Schol, bishop, New Jersey Episcopal Area, The UMC

"I am often asked, 'What would John Wesley say to United Methodists today about our divisions and disagreements?' While this is an impossible question to answer, Bishop Carter captures better than anything I have seen Wesley's deep commitment to both the authority of scripture and the necessity of reading scripture in conversation with one another, ever open to the leading of the Spirit. And, like Wesley, Carter writes from a deeply pastoral heart."

—Randy L. Maddox, William Kellon Quick Professor of Wesleyan and Methodist Studies, Duke Divinity School, Duke University, Durham, NC

"Blessed are the peacemakers. Ken Carter looms large among United Methodists, as president of the Council of Bishops and a moderators of the Commission on the Way Forward—and because he leads with a quiet, empathetic grace. *Embracing the Wideness* should be read and studied as a Wesleyan way forward. A call to 'fear not' in the wilderness in which we find ourselves."

—David McAllister-Wilson, president, Wesley Theological Seminary, Washington, DC

"Ken Carter is more than just an extraordinary leader and a gifted communicator. He is a much-needed pacifist in the culture war and an exceptional advocate for generous orthodoxy. In a bitterly divided time, *Embracing the Wideness* calls us to rediscover—with humility, awe, and camaraderie—God's grace for all people."

—Magrey R. deVega, senior pastor, Hyde Park United Methodist Church, Tampa, FL; author, *One Faithful Promise: The Wesleyan Covenant Renewal*, *Embracing the Uncertain*, and *Awaiting the Already*

"At certain points when reading this book I wanted to shout, 'This is The United Methodist Church I know and love!' In these pages the people of The United Methodist Church are invited to cross a bridge that draws us closer to one another and closer to God. Over and under and all around that bridge flow streams of scripture and song and story—streams of grace and mercy never ceasing."

—Ginger E. Gaines-Cirelli, senior pastor (she/her/hers), Foundry UMC, Washington, DC

"In a season of polarization and a climate that accents differences, *Embracing the Wideness* draws its readers together in a deeply biblical and theological exploration of a generous Wesleyan orthodoxy. One of our most thoughtful bishops, Ken Carter writes with the convicted humility of a long-time pastor, preacher, and church leader."

—Janice Riggle Huie, retired bishop, South Central Jurisdiction, The UMC

"In this book, Bishop Ken Carter uses the concept of generous orthodoxy to transcend the dueling positions of traditionalist or progressive and seek instead the 'third way.' This is a must-read book as we head into our 2019 Special Called Session of the General Conference."

—Grant Hagiya, bishop, Western Jurisdiction of The UMC; author, *Spiritual Kaizen*

FOREWORD

How typical of Ken Carter to see a church crisis as an opportunity to preach and as a call for Wesleyan theology. Bishop Carter is as good a pastoral theologian as we have among United Methodist bishops. Ken's strong, Christ-committed voice can lead us in thinking about the present moment like Christians and in being a more faithful church.

Recently one of us had a phone call from a longtime friend who is also a longtime Baptist pastor in a moderate-sized town in East Texas. That's not the sort of place where one would expect to find many who might identify with what is often thought to be liberal causes. I asked him how the church was, expecting a general response of, "It's tough, but we are hanging in there." Instead he said they were doing very well. He was especially pleased that they had attracted a number of young families of mixed race. He then reported on one of the families he praised as having wonderful parents determined to give their children a distinctively Christian formation. He added that both of the parents are women.

That's the reality we take to be the driving force behind Ken Carter's impassioned book that tries to help Methodists stay true to their deepest Christian convictions *and* find a way to recognize the reality of Christians who happen to be gay. Here is Wesleyan conjunctive theology at its best—Christ and the church together into the future. The challenge before Bishop Carter is how to

PREFACE

For twenty-eight years I was a pastor and preacher in local churches. During this season I lived in the tension of these two callings: to care for the flock of God that had been given to me through the assignment of my bishop, and to interpret the scriptures with and for those gathered each week in the sanctuary for worship and in smaller groups for study.

And so I approach this conversation—about the unity of the church, a way forward, and LGBTQ identity—as a pastor and a preacher whom God called, through the laity and clergy of a jurisdictional conference, to the work of oversight (*episkopos*, bishop) for a season.

This season happens to be one in which the tensions are more pronounced than those I experienced in local churches. I no longer serve a parish, but rather a large and diverse annual conference (Florida) and, at the calling of colleague bishops, as president of the Council of Bishops of The United Methodist Church. I have also recently concluded work as one of the moderators of the Commission on a Way Forward, and my experience with that global body shaped this book.

And yet, even as the context of my ministry has changed, my fundamental vocation remains the same: to be a preacher and a pastor, to be an interpreter of texts and, at the same time, an interpreter of the lives of the people God has sent to us. At

GENEROUS ORTHODOXY AND THE PEOPLE CALLED METHODIST

Matthew 18

---+---

My faith has been formed by:

- reading the New Testament from beginning to end, one spring

- singing in choirs as a youth and young adult

- serving on mission trips

- memorizing scripture with the Navigators as a college student

- witnessing a public request for forgiveness

- seeing racism diminish in people I admired

- teachers who came along at just the right time

- experiencing the courage of clergywomen who kept going even when no one affirmed them of *Christianity Today*. I don't know if there is a voice between these two, as a matter of fact. If there is, I would like to pursue it."[2]

Generous Orthodoxy is the title of a blog by the brilliant Episcopal preacher and priest Fleming Rutledge, who writes,

> We cannot do without orthodoxy, for everything else must be tested against it, but that orthodox (traditional, classical) Christian faith should by definition always be generous as our God is generous; lavish in his creation, binding himself in an unconditional covenant, revealing himself in the calling of a people, self-sacrificing in the death of his Son, prodigal in the gifts of the Spirit, justifying the ungodly, and, indeed, offending the "righteous" by the indiscriminate use of his favor. True Christian orthodoxy therefore cannot be narrow, pinched or defensive but always spacious, adventurous and unafraid.[3]

More recently, "Generous Orthodoxy" was the title of a Malcolm Gladwell *Revisionist History* podcast. Gladwell tells the story of a same-gender wedding in the Mennonite Church tradition, and how that community navigated the claims of received truth and expressed conscience. The story itself is narrated in a gracious way, especially given the medium of popular culture. In his own reflection on the events narrated in the podcast, Gladwell notes that "You must respect the body you are trying to heal."[4]

What great things God could accomplish if we rediscovered an orthodoxy in service of the healing (and not dividing) of our bodies, that is, our churches?[5] Such a generous orthodoxy would help us not to become immersed in the emotional processes that pit people against each other. Such a generous orthodoxy would keep us from becoming stuck in cycles of harmful collusion and escalating conflict.[6]

Such a generous orthodoxy would know that the source of our capacity to be healed of our schisms is a miracle beyond our human power or goodness or intelligence.

Empathy

I empathize with those who do not see or hold the faith as I do. My way is not the superior way or the only way. I believe, however, because of experiences, teachers, relationships, and vocational calling that this is the way God has given me to walk.

Because my faith is orthodox, I can learn from and listen to voices many would characterize as moderate, evangelical, catholic, and traditional. These theological streams have always been life-giving to me.[7]

Because my faith is generously orthodox, I believe that the heart and soul of orthodoxy is grace. This grace is a broad, deep river, a wide reservoir of divine love, a fountain filled with blood that cleanses my unrighteousness and overcomes all of my resistance and rebellion. It is a grace greater than all my sin. And this grace is for all people. Note the words of Charles Wesley:

> Teach me to cast thy net aright,
>   the gospel net of general grace,
>   so shall I *all* to thee invite,
>   and draw them to their Lord's embrace,
>   within Thine arms of love include
>   and catch a willing multitude.[8]

Note the prominence of the word *all* throughout the body of Charles Wesley's hymns; for example:

observes "that conflict is a part and parcel of Christian unity means that the unity of a church is not a unity based on agreements, but rather one that assumes that disagreements should not lead to division but rather should be a testimony to the existence of a reconciling people."[10]

What if orthodoxy is not the elimination of our differences but the calling to live together faithfully in the midst of them? In seeking to visualize what a generous orthodoxy might look like, in practice, consider a simple drawing of three circles to portray something of where we are as a church in the present moment.

Image of Circles

The three circles are *covenant*, *justice*, and *unity*, and I visualize them as coming together to create an overlapping space, not unlike a Venn diagram.[11]

Covenantal people greatly value the promises we have made to God and to each other in baptism, in ordination, and in consecration. They seek greater public accountability when our covenants are broken.

Those in a search for *justice* participate in a history that gives greater rights and offers God's grace and blessings to more people. This history includes the abolition of slavery, the recognition of women in ministry, and now the inclusion of the LGBTQ community in the full life of the church.

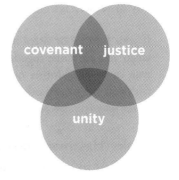

Those who value *unity* hold the conviction that covenantal people and justice seekers can live together in the church. They do not see the present LGBTQ conversation as a church-dividing issue, and they live in the tension, often at the congregational level, amidst differences that reflect the beauty and complexity of the one body.

My own calling is to seek to *expand* or *grow* the space where these three circles *overlap*.[12] I share passions of justice, covenant, and unity with friends across my own annual conference and the global church. The shared space where justice, covenant, and unity overlap is *not* a mushy middle! It is the complex place where many faithful people live. It is the practical divinity that flows from a generous orthodoxy.

✚

The Center

What if the center is not a mushy middle but the cross of Jesus that is strong enough to hold the tension of the opposites?

The vision of the Commission on a Way Forward is to "design a way for being church that maximizes the presence of a United Methodist witness in as many places in the world as possible, that allows for as much contextual differentiation as possible, and that balances an approach to different theological understandings of human sexuality with a desire for as much unity as possible."[13]

I understand this to be the generative work of our denomination in this present moment. And this generative work is possible through the theological resources of a generous orthodoxy.

In his book *Recapturing the Wesleys' Vision*, Paul Chilcote describes our tradition as a "place" that is not "either/or" but "both/ and." "The Wesleyan method," he writes, "can be called conjunctive because it seeks to join things together, rather than permitting them to be pulled apart."[14] And so he speaks of faith and works, personal and social, heart and head, Christ and culture, piety and mercy.

This is The United Methodist Church in its most local and global expression. At our best we are connected to each other for a purpose: "to make disciples of Jesus Christ for the transformation of the world." This mission includes keeping covenant, loving justice, and seeking unity. And it is about growing, expanding, and honoring the space where these three values can be joined together.

The recovery of a generously orthodox faith matters. When we are generous, we are not closed off from each other. This is for our good. When we are orthodox, we are in a right relationship with the God who speaks, is incarnate, and breathes in scripture and in our own lives. This is our salvation. And this is the church's mission that is "spacious, adventurous and unafraid." If we know the history of how God has moved for millennia over the face of this creation, why would we imagine that the renewal, reform, and healing of the church would not be a recovery of how we think about God and how we therefore live in transformed ways with each other? And if we were reading the signs of the times, why would we not trust that this same God was and is in Christ reconciling the world to himself and that God has given us—The United Methodist Church—this ministry of reconciliation (2 Cor 5)?[15]

A Conviction

I continue to hold the conviction that a generous Christian orthodoxy—grounded in scripture and tradition, faithfully lived and taught by the church at its best—is broad and deep enough to transform the brittle and harsh political and sociological captivity that so easily lures the church with its siren voice. Finally, there is no conservative or liberal agenda worthy of Colossians 1 or Romans 12 or Psalm 139 or Ephesians 2 or Matthew 25. Our own gospel of justice and mercy is like treasure, hidden in a field, waiting to be rediscovered.

Chapter Two

CONFESSING AND RECONCILING

Ephesians 2

uring the interview for serving as a bishop, and when consecrated and later installed, a sentence stayed with me from the *Book of Discipline* and *Book of Worship*:

A bishop is called to guard the faith,
> to seek the unity and to exercise the discipline of the whole Church.

In one moment along the way, I was asked, in front of a large group of committed, invested, diverse, faithful, and, indeed, exhausted Christian people, "Will you accept the call to this ministry as a bishop and fulfill this trust in obedience to Christ?"

And I responded,

I will, by the grace of God.

As the work unfolded over several years, again and again a passage of scripture, Ephesians 2, connects with this work-in-progress, which is the essence of a Christian life and the grounding for a role and office of a bishop:

You are saved by God's grace because of your faith. This salvation is God's gift. It's not something you possessed. It's not something you did that you can be proud of. (CEB)

Those verses, Ephesians 2:8-9, written either by Paul or someone who wrote, thought, and sounded very much like Paul, summarizes an extended argument about the journey from the old life to the new. In the words of an old saying,

I'm not what I want to be,
I'm not what I am going to be,
but thank God I'm not what I used to be!

All of us once lived in destructive ways, the letter says, and then there is the turning point, in Ephesians 2:4: "But God…" It is a clue to leave the past behind and focus on the future.

Years ago, I recall watching a televised conversation with the pundit William Bennett, who was campaigning for Dan Quayle, who at the time was seeking political office in the United States. Bennett had been deeply critical of Dan Quayle in an earlier time but had come around, as they say, and so the commentator was asking how all of this could have happened. Bennett reflected for a moment and then responded, "Every saint has a past and every sinner has a future."

All of us used to act like most people in the world do. We followed the rule of a destructive spiritual power. "But God…"

Yes, every saint has a past (this keeps us humble), but every sinner has a future. And that is all about the grace of God, who is rich in mercy. This is the very same God who raised us from the dead to live in Christ. We are saved by grace, through faith, and this is a gift.

This is the faith we confess. And so what would it be like to have a movement within our church that is a *confessing movement*? We would depend on the grace of God that saves us. We would be honest about our flaws and confident in the One who heals us.

We could end there with confession, but the scripture does not end there, and our work—our individual work, our work in congregations, our work as a denomination—does not end there. Paul moves forward to describe this faith not only at a personal level but from a corporate perspective.

Often, in life, people form into two groups. My first pastoral appointment was to a four-point charge. Two of the congregations were Prospect and New Home, located within sight of each other in a very rural community. New Home was actually the "New Home" of Prospect. They had divided after the Civil War, although no one could remember the actual reason. I asked how they were distinct from each other. "Oh," one of matriarchs said, "Prospect is a democrat church, and New Home is a republican church."

We continue building these dividing walls of hostility— choose your style of worship, the color of your state, or your tribal tradition. In *Healing the Heart of Democracy,* Parker Palmer observes our "issue silos."[1] Polarization goes back a long way, even in the family of God. And so Paul could not conclude with the glorious good news of our personal salvation; there was unfinished business. He had to remind these two groups that they were *one* in Christ. A part of this missionary and apostolic calling was to seek the unity.

This remains our unfinished business. The words are fresh in my memory, because I can recall saying them a few short years ago: I would not only *guard the faith*, I would *seek the unity*.

This bias for unity is countercultural. It would be possible to preach a sermon on unity from a partisan spirit or to hear a sermon on unity and take it in a divisive direction. An article in the *United Methodist Reporter*, written by Jack Jackson, an elder from my own episcopal area who teaches at one of our theological schools, came to the conclusion that "Breaking Up Is Hard, But the Right Thing for The United Methodist Church."[2]

The article is clearly argued and somewhat persuasive. And yet I am stirred within to seek something else. I served those two rural churches within sight of each other. I have sat in the body of the General Conference a few times. I know about "issue silos."

What if there were not only a confessing movement within our church but also a *reconciling movement*? And what would be the basis of that reconciliation? It is, I believe, grounded in the same realities of grace and gift.

We stand in a tradition with a deep and abiding sense of grace, because our God is rich in mercy. In our theological reading of scripture we affirm:

- God's *prevenient grace*: that we are created in the image of God, every one of us, and that sin mars and disfigures this image but never destroys it.

- God's *justifying grace*: that we are saved by grace through faith, that the ground is level at the foot of the cross and we kneel there with open hands and hearts to receive the gift. And in that moment we are bold to claim the language of Paul in Galatians 2:20 (CEB), "I have been crucified with Christ and I no longer live, but Christ lives in me. And the life that I now live in my body, I live by faith, indeed, by the faithfulness of God's Son, who loved me and gave himself for me." We say yes to the gift, but we must continue to say yes daily.

- God's *sanctifying grace*: once we have claimed a common dignity toward each other, and once we have embraced a common humility within ourselves, before God, we are moved to continue the journey toward holiness, perfection, the restoration of the image of God. This holiness, we know is personal (not impersonal) and social (not antisocial).[3]

At our worst we often want to divide the gift, as if we could, as if this were an option, to create a personal holiness camp and a social justice club, a right wing and a left wing, a republican church and a democrat church, a confessing movement and a reconciling movement. And so some talk about truth and unity, as if they could be divided, and most often as if unity is the stepchild of truth.

But what if the fullness of the gospel is confessing *and* reconciling? What if the fullness of the gospel is my own personal experience of a grace that saves me and takes me from the old life to the new life (Eph 2:8) *and* my inescapable participation (Eph 2:14) in the breaking down of the dividing wall of hostility that separates me from my brother and my sister?

This is more than "let's just get along." It is more than tolerance. It is even more than inclusivity! It is the fullness of the gospel; it is the mystery of grace.

In the call of the church to serve as a bishop, we are asked and we promise to work on this unfinished business of confessing and reconciling and overcoming hostility with grace.

As one of the moderators of the Commission on a Way Forward, I spent a great deal of time with the people of our local churches and with stakeholders across the connection. And I would often hear more than a few of them saying, in their own way, "Breaking up is hard to do, but it is the right thing for The United Methodist Church. Don't you think that is where we are headed, Bishop?"

Sometimes I wonder. And then I remember the words I often find myself saying each morning, words found in the *Book of Common Prayer*:

> Lord Jesus Christ,
> you stretched out your arms of love on the hard wood of the
> cross
>> that everyone might come within the reach of your saving
>> embrace:
> So clothe us in your Spirit
>> that we, reaching forth our hands in love,
>> may bring those who do not know you
>> to the knowledge and love of you;
>> for the honor of your Name.

So, why are we going to guard the faith and seek the unity of the church? Because we made that promise and, yes, there is integrity in inhabiting the role. Because of who we are and what the church has asked us to do, there are days we find ourselves stretching out our arms of love on the hard wood of some cross, leadership taking the shape of a cruciform life.[4] So we remember our callings. In one way or another, through the providence of God and the will of the church, bishops are asked or called or persuaded to do it. This is who we are, and this is where we find ourselves.

Come Holy Spirit

But the call to guard the faith and seek the unity surely goes deeper than the current climate of church and culture, or a decision that flows from the majority will of a General Conference. It is grounded in the nature of God who is One. It is the prayer of Jesus for his disciples in John 17. We often echo this prayer as we prepare to come to the Lord's table.

In The United Methodist Church the minister stands at the altar, raises his or her hands to God, and says the words of the epiclesis, the invocation that the Holy Spirit will be present in the bread and the cup that we receive, the body of Christ, and that we will actually be the body of Christ in the world. And then the powerful request of God: to make us one with Christ (faithfulness), one with each other (unity), and one in ministry to all the world (fruitfulness).

A sacramental minister of the gospel is licensed or ordained for this purpose: to see that the work of the Holy Spirit does sustain ordinary people—that is, all of us—in our daily attempt to represent Christ wherever we are. The faithfulness, unity, and fruitfulness of the church form a whole. We cannot be one without abiding in Jesus. We cannot be spirit-filled without loving our neighbor. And we cannot experience revival as we sow divisions within the body.

> Make us one with Christ,
>   one with each other,
>   and one in ministry to all the world.

———————————— ✚ ————————————

Is there a future with hope? In ourselves? Maybe not. In our issue silos? Surely not.

But God...
You are saved by God's grace because of your faith.
This salvation is God's gift.
> It's not something you possessed.
> It's not something you did that you can be proud of.
Instead, we are God's accomplishment,
> created in Christ Jesus to do good things.
God planned for these good things to be the way that we live our lives....
But now, thanks to Christ Jesus, you who once were so far away
> have been brought near by the blood of Christ.
Christ is our peace....
With his body, he broke down the barrier of hatred that divided us.
He canceled the detailed rules of the Law
> so that he could create one new person out of the two groups, making peace.
He reconciled them both as one body to God by the cross...
> (Eph 2:8-16 CEB)

SO FREE, SO INFINITE HIS GRACE

Luke 15

I admire the parable of Jesus that we have named "The Prodigal Son." It may be Jesus's best-known teaching. Along with most pastors, I've preached the parable many times. I often chose this parable at homecomings, especially in small membership and town and country churches, which included for a day the adult children who had migrated into urban lives.

So the story begins. A man had two sons. The rabbis said this is a clue that something bad is going to happen. The stories throughout the book of Genesis are based on sibling rivalry. Adam had two sons. Isaac had two sons. Well, the younger son goes to far country and squanders everything. Don't be too hard on the younger brother. Have we not all squandered something? A gift, an opportunity, an inheritance?

In the far country, the youngest child hits bottom. Life becomes degrading, a violation of the child's humanity. We see human degradation in every culture. People around the world, especially women and children, are trapped in the sin of human trafficking.

And there, in that moment, the child "came to his senses." It is a conversion. In life there are many conversions. When we come to our senses, when we "find our self," we recognize that we are created in God's image. And in our Wesleyan theology, God's image is never lost. Perhaps it is defaced or disfigured, but it is never lost. There is something of God in every one of us.

The question is, how do we recover it?

According to John Wesley, "The first step in this glorious change is humility; a knowledge of ourselves, a just sense of our condition."[1]

To hit bottom is literally to be *grounded*! And so, there, in that moment, the son says, "I will get up and go to my father!"

It is a resurrection.

It is an Easter.

It is the discovery, or the memory, that we can go home.

And here the focus of the story shifts—from the son to the *father*. The father is watching, his eyes fixed a long way off. We see what we are looking for. And the father runs and *embraces* the child.

Why does the father run?

There are at least two possible explanations, and neither rules out the other. The parent loves the child. And also, perhaps, in an honor and shame culture, the parent runs to protect the returning child from the community, who would likely retaliate for the humiliation the son caused in the first place by claiming the inheritance and departing.

On the way home, the son has been rehearsing the speech: "Father, I have sinned against heaven and against you. I no longer deserve to be called your son. Take me on as one of your hired hands" (Luke 15:18-19). The son begins the speech, but strikingly never gets to give it.

Such is the unconditional love of God. The father interrupts: kill the calf, bring the robe and ring. The child was dead and is alive, lost and is found! And they begin to celebrate!

It is quite a story, but this is not the whole story. What if, on the way home, the younger brother had met the older brother first? We remember that there are *two* sons.

The older brother hears the celebration, inquires, and refuses to go into the house. Try not be too hard on the older brother. I am an older child. In preaching this passage, I have sometimes asked a congregation, "How many of you are an older child in your family?" Almost always a large number of hands go up. Oldest children are conscientious; we get things done. Someone has to run the farm. Someone has to take responsibility. Someone has to serve on a committee. Someone has to keep the lights on in a local church!

There is a celebration! But the older brother will simply have none of it. Now, we might wonder, "Who is lost?" And the father says to the older sibling, "You are always with me." With Henri Nouwen we know that the father loves both children equally.

So, what does this story teach us about God? God is like the waiting parent. And Jesus is the son who goes into the far country. He descends into hell. An early church hymn reflects this demeaned condition: "Though he was in the form of God, he did not consider being equal with God something to exploit" (Phil 2:6). Compare the words of Charles Wesley in his hymn, "And Can It Be":

He left his Father's throne above
   (so free, so infinite his grace!),
emptied himself of all but love,

and bled for Adam's helpless race.
'Tis mercy all, immense and free,
for O my God, it found out me![2]

The story tells us about God's nature and character. And the story has a context. Jesus gave this parable in response to questions about his own life and leadership. There were complaints and criticisms, which had perhaps gone viral!

And these are stated clearly in Luke 15:2: "This man welcomes sinners and eats with them." Jesus is teaching us about the divine nature and character. At a practical level, we begin to learn about the free and infinite grace of God and express it in our own contexts.

It is first a complicated grace, because our lives are in this parable. There is the self-loathing, self-condemnation of experience in the far country. There is the judgmentalism and criticism in a life of rigorous duty and stability. There is shame and guilt, envy and comparison. Our lives are in this parable, and the lives of our people, corporately, are in this parable.

It is a grace that comes to us in the midst of criticism and complaint. Jesus responds to criticism by telling three stories that have, at their heart, the experience of joy. The recurring refrain in Luke 15:6 and 15:9 is "Rejoice with me!" How do our congregations rejoice? When someone is baptized? When someone makes a public profession of faith in Christ, or renews their faith? Many of our congregations never see this happen. And so perhaps we are called to go out to where the "others" are.

There is also in the parable a sense of grace and joy in the small things. We have a resistance to living a joyful life, particularly when we form into coalitions, and adopt a way of thinking characterized by polarizing labels such as "liberals" and "conservatives."

Liberals are often cynical.

Conservatives are often suspicious.

And so we bond over a hermeneutic of cynicism and suspicion. Neither contributes to a joyful life. Henri Nouwen's suggestion is that we rejoice in small things. God rejoices when one sheep is found, when one coin is found, when one child is found. All is not perfect, or just, or pure. But the voice of God says "rejoice with me."

Rejoice with Me!

If the church is to know the fruit of the spirit that is joy, we will know that we include in our fellowship younger and older siblings, both prodigals and those who have never left—and that God loves them equally! And this is the free and infinite grace of God!

Some of us are...

- in the far country. Nouwen describes this as in itinerant ministry, our constant activity.

- ready to come to our senses, to ourselves, and to discover or rediscover our spiritual center. Where is home?

- the waiting parent, living in the tension of being a spiritual leader with those who have wandered away and with those who resent them.

- ready to celebrate, ready to rediscover our joy.

- eager to proclaim the good news: the lost are found, the unholy are made holy, the unrighteous are made righteous by the blood of his cross.

This is a story about the grace of God. A lively conversation in the church continues about grace and the relation of grace to holiness. It is an appropriate conversation that is in the Gospels as well.

The early Christian communities circulated two particular sayings of Jesus that pertain to this conversation, from the Sermon on the Mount (Matthew) or the Sermon on the Plain (Luke). These are his challenges, to the disciples, and to us:

> "Be perfect, therefore, as your heavenly Father is perfect" (Matt 5:48 NRSV). The word for "perfect" is *telos*, or "complete," as in reaching an end, which is the basis for the CEB: "Just as your heavenly Father is complete in showing love to everyone, so also you must be complete."

> "Be compassionate, just as your Father is compassionate" (Luke 6:36 CEB). The word for compassion is *oiktirmon*, or mercy.

In the Gospels there is an obvious relationship between *perfection* (or completion) in love and *compassion*. Can there be holiness apart from grace? Could it be that they describe one reality about God's character? And that our separation of holiness from grace is artificial?

I am like the son who goes into the far country...and here I relate in my own itineracy from a mill town to Virginia for graduate school to a rural parish to churches in three cities and then to the mountains of Western North Carolina and later to Florida.

I see myself in the older brother, in my judgment and critique of others. I sometimes wonder about others: *Why aren't they more successful or fruitful or focused or loyal or disciplined?*

And I see myself in the father. I read *Return of the Prodigal Son* by Henri Nouwen over thirty years ago. At that point, my identity was informed by the sons in the story. I am now sixty years old, and the questions are different: How can I be at peace with all of the younger and older siblings in my life, and seek to bless them and say, "You are always with me"? Nouwen names this as his discovery. Writing four years prior to his death, he claimed this as the season to be a compassionate father.

This parable in the Gospels also speaks to our present-day sibling rivalry in The United Methodist Church. The spiritual leader in the parable is the father (although, in Rembrandt's painting[3] and in Nouwen's reflection, one hand is masculine and one is feminine). The father is both passive (waiting) and active (blessing). The father is in relationship to the younger and oldest sons (children). Each has a different history, each has displayed distinct behaviors.

The oldest children are with us too. They are good, loyal, diligent people. Some have spent at least seven years in higher education, learning about God. Many of these become clergy, they wear robes, they keep up with the statistics. They know who has been present and who has been missing.

The oldest children have probably spent some time writing the rules of the church, or voting on them, or evaluating clergy, or approving the credentials of clergy, or grading students, or voting on tenure, or forwarding legal motions. Or thinking about the weighty matter of what is just or unjust.

As I age through wisdom and experience, I identify with the spiritual parent. I have journeyed and itinerated, like the younger son. I have been dutiful, responsible, critical, and even resentful, like the older son. But in the family system, I do not quite function in the roles of the son—I am more like the parent. The system needs me to be a parent. What does this mean?

I certainly serve a church of younger and older siblings. Some are in the embrace of God's unconditional love. Some are still in the far country. Some are on the way home, but at some distance. Some are within sight of home. What will the reception be like, should they make it home?

In the parable, it is not clear whether the younger and older child are reconciled. And yet there is a celebration. There is a feast. There is a banquet.

So it is always a complicated grace.

And so I encourage the people called Methodist, especially in the United Methodist expression of that, to...

- Live in the grace of God, even in the midst of criticism and complaint. On your most difficult days in ministry and service, you will need to return to the anchor that is grace.

- Find the gift of God's grace, even in the small things. This is the blessing of ministry with ordinary people, people like us.

- Lean into the free and infinite grace of a God who loves all kinds of people.

DISCERNING THE MOVEMENT OF THE HOLY SPIRIT AMIDST DEEP CULTURAL CHANGE

Acts 15

How do leaders navigate change? How do clergy and pastors navigate change? How do congregations and denominations navigate change? Of course, a disciple turns to scripture to answer these questions. It is true that scripture is a foundation on which we stand; it is true, as we sang in the church of my childhood, that Christ is the solid rock on which we stand, and all other ground is sinking sand. All other ground is sinking sand.

I know that hymn by heart. And yet it is also true that scripture documents the movement of God's people in the midst of change. Abraham and Sarah are called to go to a new country. Moses is called to lead the people out of slavery. We hear the voice of Isaiah, calling the people to return home. Mary is obedient to the Word as she is called to give birth to the Savior. Jesus commands the disciples to leave everything and follow him.

And then we venture through the book of Acts. Luke describes the movement (and yes, movement always implies change) of the Holy Spirit in the lives of the witnesses to Jesus's life, death, and resurrection. "You will be my witnesses [*martyrs*] in Jerusalem, in all Judea and Samaria, and to the end of the earth" (Acts 1:8 CEB). If we are going to make that journey, we will learn to navigate change. The lives of the earliest leaders in the Way, Peter and Paul, are turned upside down. They learn to navigate change.

I don't presume to speak for you, but most of us prefer the status quo. We adapt to the status quo. Change requires a great deal of energy, and it is disruptive. Some change is thrust upon us. Some change we choose, almost reluctantly. Some change is inevitable: we get older, our parents age, and our children grow up. And some change seems to be within the plan and purpose of God. Conversion is change. Surrender is change. To "renounce the spiritual forces of wickedness, reject the evil powers of this world and repent of our sin"[1] is change. To walk into newness of life is change.

But none of us, if we are honest, like change. I remember one group facilitator saying, "I love change. I love it when *other* people change!"

Bearing Witness to Change

It is within the primary task of the preacher to proclaim the need for change, to teach about change, to appeal to others to change, and to live through some change in our own lives. Think, for a moment, about a change you have lived through. I recall a moment of change that had a profound effect on me. I was in the church of my childhood, in the deep South, and we were in a Sunday evening service. We were nearing the end of the service. As on most Sunday nights, the gathered congregation was rather sparse. The preacher asked if anyone had a word of testimony before we had the closing prayer. I was praying that no one would speak up. It had probably been a long day—Sunday school, morning worship, youth in the afternoon, evening service. The end was in sight!

"Does anyone have a word of testimony?"

There was a silence, as usual. On most Sunday evenings, no one spoke. But then someone interrupted the silence. His name was Bob, and he was a pillar of the church. I also knew Bob to be one of the kindest men in that church. Later, as a teenager, I would work in a grocery store after school and on weekends. Bob was a representative for a brand of cookies. I don't want to characterize our crew, at the grocery store, but we were a group in need of transformation, change, conversion. Let's leave it there!

And yet, when Bob entered the store, it was as if something did, in fact, change. There was a light, a joy, a compassion, a spirit of holiness that infused our environment. I did not have that kind of language for it at the time, but that was the effect. He was a disciple of Jesus Christ who transformed the world. In this instance, it happened to be our grocery store.

That Sunday evening, years ago, it happened, of all places, in the sanctuary. Bob asked to share a brief word of testimony. He said very simply and clearly:

> I have lived a long life, I have lived in this community, and I have been a part of this church for most of my life. I genuinely love all of you. And this evening I want to say that I have been completely wrong about the subject of race, and how we live with people of another skin color. This evening, I repent of that. And if God is speaking to you, I invite you to do the same.

In that moment there was silence. And next a closing prayer, I suppose, and then we walked out into the dark night of the south Georgia sky. But something had happened. Call it conversion, call it transformation, call it change. For me it was a turning point.

God does change us.

Change Comes to the Early Church

Acts 15 is a turning point in the scriptures, and in it the leaders (apostles) come to grips with the implications of all that has been happening since Acts 10, which records the gift of the Holy Spirit to the Gentiles and their conversion. The shift in momentum in those chapters is remarkable.

In Acts 13–14, the tension builds: the Gentiles are responding to the good news, the Jewish leaders are filled with jealousy (13:45), and there are clear divisions: "some siding with the Jews, others with the Lord's messengers" (14:4). The stage is set for some kind of resolution.

- The expansion: An angel of the Lord speaks to Cornelius by name and gives him a vision (10:3).

- Peter has a dream in which the Lord speaks to him and says, "Never consider unclean what God has made pure" (10:15 CEB).

- Peter says, upon meeting Cornelius, "God has shown me that I should never call a person impure or unclean" (10:28 CEB).

- When the Gentiles receive the power of the Holy Spirit, Peter baptizes them (10:48).

- When the Jewish leaders hear about this, they are critical. Peter responds, "Never consider unclean what God has made pure" (11:9 CEB).

- It is the Holy Spirit, Peter says, that has told him not to make a distinction between them and us (11:12).

And those who are witnesses acknowledge, "So then God has enabled Gentiles to change their hearts and lives so that they might have new life" (11:18 CEB). According to Paul and Barnabas, God has "opened a door of faith for the Gentiles" (14:27 NRSV). And yet, as with all powerful missional movements, there is a counterreaction, from "certain individuals"—mercifully, Luke allows them to remain anonymous—individuals who have a problem with this trend: circumcision in the custom (Greek: *ethos*) of Moses is required for salvation. As you know, there is change, and there is resistance to change. Do you remember the scientific principle: for every action, there is an equal and opposite reaction?

Yet, there is no denying the reality that change is taking place. And so this leads to a summit—Paul and Barnabas go "up" to Jerusalem to talk about this with the apostles (namely Peter) and the elders. The remainder of the chapter is the report of that meeting. And those gathered seem to be of two minds: those who are delighted with the reports of Gentile conversions, and those (Pharisees) who are not.

The primary witnesses are Peter, Paul, and Barnabas. It is interesting that in Acts this does mark a shift in narration; Peter, so prominent in the earlier chapters, becomes less central to the movement, and Paul especially comes to be acknowledged as the primary leader.

Peter reminds them that God has given them the Holy Spirit, and that God makes no distinction between Jew and Gentile (Acts 10:34 CEB—"God doesn't show partiality to one group of people over another"—a lectionary passage often read on Easter Sunday). Salvation does not come to us through the law. "Why then are you now challenging God by placing a burden on the shoulders of these disciples that neither we nor our ancestors could bear? On the contrary, we believe that we and they are saved in the same way, by the grace of the Lord Jesus" (Acts 15:10-11 CEB).

After Paul, Barnabas, and James speak, it is discerned that the Gentiles do not have to be circumcised.[2] Because it "seemed good to the Holy Spirit and us" (15:28), they are given four instructions (15:20), including the call to abstain from sexual immorality (*porneia*).[3] Luke Johnson connects this command with the objection of making idols as a ritual practice, because the making of idols leads to *porneia*.[4] As in most cultures, sexuality becomes an idol. Luke Johnson summarizes the purpose of Acts 15 clearly: "the human church now catches up with the divine initiative, and formally declares itself to be on the side of God's plan to save all humanity." There is also a way of honoring tradition without making it essential for salvation; this is the difference between grace and law, and this will be the subject in a later epistle that Paul writes to the Galatians.

Change Comes to the Late Modern Church

There are three lessons for us in the experience of the early Christian leaders.

First, had the Jerusalem Council decided that circumcision was essential for salvation, Christianity would today likely have become a subset of Judaism (not unlike one of the branches of that faith: conservative, reformed, orthodox, reconstructionist, Hasidic). Instead we are part of the tree of life whose roots are in Israel (Rom 9–11), with the understanding that some traditions (*ethos*, customs) can be laid aside. This decision allowed the church to become *catholic* and *apostolic*. This decision also allowed for the missionary adaptation to the larger world with only the core essentials of grace and faith as indispensable to relationship with the One God and fellowship with each other.

A wise missionary pastor discerns, in any situation, that there is a difference between what is essential and what can be laid aside. And of course, this is the point of conflict: what is a matter of indifference to one person may be essential to her neighbor. In this context the practices of wisdom and discernment, listening and speaking the truth in love, and listening some more and arriving at a decision take place.

Second, the process of discernment gave clear priority to the eyewitnesses who had observed the power of the Holy Spirit in the lives of an unlikely group, the Gentiles. This would later be true, in our Wesleyan movement, as a basis for the role of women as evangelists, and, to state the point modestly, it is true now in the presence of the Holy Spirit in the lives of disciples of Jesus who are gay and lesbian in their orientation. Of course, how that identity relates to *porneia* is a different question, just as it is an essential question for heterosexual identity.[5]

There is a diversity of thought about the identities and stories of homosexual persons in our church. Yet my sense is that most of us have been eyewitnesses to grace among persons of LGBTQ identity; we have seen the presence of God, through the power of the Holy Spirit, in the lives of gay and lesbian Christians. I have been an eyewitness to this reality.

Acts 15 is an often-quoted chapter on many sides of the question. Luke Johnson and Bill Arnold have each written about this chapter in the Bible.[6] A part of our challenge is to recognize this as one implication for teaching Acts 15, but not to lose sight of its larger relevance for us.

Third, the gift of Acts 15 to the church and to leaders today is a thorough account of discernment on a key issue that faced the church about which there was disagreement. The issue (circumcision) could not be ignored, and indeed the answer would shape and determine implications for the future mission. The apostles give us a model for behavior in seeking the will of God, and in attending to what they are seeing with their own eyes and touching with their own hands (1 John 1), and, finally, they were given a word: *"it seemed good to the Holy Spirit and (therefore) to us."*

In the end, the disciples are flexible in strategy but united in core practices of discipleship. The law is not abolished, but we certainly sense, in Jesus's teaching, and now in the apostles' discernment, a necessary revision of the law. Jesus comes not to abolish the law but to fulfill it (Matt 5:17). And the apostles now have the leadership question thrust upon them: How do we interpret ancient teachings and practices in a missionary landscape undergoing deep change?

A strategy was required of them. The strategy is related to questions of custom and ethos. The union is about essentials. It is noteworthy that the leaders gather together, they listen to the movement of the Holy Spirit, and the result is change. They lay aside something that was, for over a thousand years, a core practice, an outward and visible sign of obedience to the Torah: circumcision. Circumcision was fundamental to the identity of God's people. And yet it was an external mark of something that was internal.

Cultural Change, Human Sexuality, and the Church

As we navigate change in a crucial time in the history of the church—and not only for United Methodists—we are often too denominationally centered in our perception of the present reality. The leaders of the Roman Catholic Church (in their Synod on the Family) and the leaders of Hillsong United, with origins in Australia, are but two branches of the global Christmas movement navigating these same changes. Communions with which we have or are exploring full communion (the Evangelical Lutheran Church, the Moravian Church, the Episcopal Church) are engaged in this discernment as well. So, what are the lessons from worldwide discernment about what seems good to the Holy Spirit and to us?

First, we are living in a period of deep cultural change. There may be a theological debate about same-gender marriage, but there is no cultural debate, and really no legislative or political debate in the United States. This may please the liberals among us.

Second, Christianity is a global church, and we are colonialist if we believe the future of our Christian faith is United States-centric. It is not. This will please the conservatives among us.

Forgive me for these labels!

Third, if we move from the thirty-thousand-feet perspective to the communities where we live and serve, we have a different set of questions. The matter shifts from issues to people: your son or daughter, your congregation's lay leader or musician, the young woman who has a gift in missions or the middle-aged man who serves on the finance committee. These are the members who have been baptized in our churches, confirmed in our churches, who serve in leadership roles in our churches, who contribute financial resources to our churches, and whose memorial services we will conduct in our churches.

The discernment asked of us is to see the movement of the Holy Spirit in the Gentiles of our own day, and to place that alongside our deepest theological convictions. And then to discern what is a custom—what can be laid aside—and what is essential. And then to act with grace in a way that does justice to each of these realities. This is the tension of being a priest and a prophet at the same time.

So, what might this look like, in practice? In a mission field, it varies from community to community. I do know that our participation in the lives of same-gender couples is a pastoral gift, even a missionary gift, just as it is with heterosexual couples. And their lives can be a gift to us. And so my bias is to look for the rather large and gracious space within our promises of ordination, and within the scriptures, and even within the *Book of Discipline*, where we can preach, pray, read the scriptures, and counsel our own people, as shepherds in a season of deep change.

Christ Alone: All Other Ground Is Sinking Sand

It strikes me that this is where the early apostles left it after the Jerusalem Council. They laid aside the customs that were not essential—but take a deep breath there, because circumcision was more than a custom for many Jewish Christians. It was a nonnegotiable commandment from scripture. And in our own time we likely do not agree about the non-negotiables—and yet we have the deeper mandate to clarify the marks of faithful discipleship. Why? Because, as Luke Johnson noted, "God has a plan to save all of humanity." So, what are the marks of faithful discipleship in our own time and place? They are listed earlier in the book, when the church exploded on the Day of Pentecost and "devoted themselves to the apostles' teaching, to the community, to their shared meals, and to their prayers" (Acts 2:42 CEB).

Acts 15 refers to something more than preaching or teaching about a controversial subject. In the tradition of John Wesley, it draws us into "preaching Christ in all his offices" as:

prophet (how we clearly proclaim the Word);

priest (how we stand in the gap with people before God and God before people);

and *king* (how we order our lives in the covenants we have made).

In his work on scripture and discernment, Luke Johnson notes that "whether Gentiles can be preached to or baptized is settled rather quickly. But the deeper human difficulty of fellowship between Jew and Gentile believers is far harder to resolve." He then asks a series of questions that are shaped by Acts 15:

If both Jews and Gentiles are to be considered part of God's people, will it be on even or uneven footing? On what basis will Gentiles be recognized and associated with? On the basis of their belief in the Messiah and the gift of the Holy Spirit, or on the basis of being circumcised and observing the law of Moses? Will the church split into two ethnically and ritually distinct bodies? Is Yahweh a tribal deity, or Lord of all?[7]

Acts 10–15 gives us a model for navigating faithful pastoral and lay leadership in a complex and changing mission context. There is a four-phase movement, from *individual experience* to *eyewitness testimony* to *discussion by mature leaders* to *discernment by the Holy Spirit*. It is the most extended model we have for the way Christ-followers think and pray their way into God's unfolding mission in a season of complexity. This is the messiness of ministry that takes us, in the command of Jesus, "from Jerusalem, to Judea and Samaria, and to the end of earth" (Acts 1:8).

And the end result, at least in the book of Acts, is a church that is both united in its communal life and growing stronger in its engagement with the world. The establishment churches must confess that, across the past fifty years, we have become more divided and more internally focused.

What Can the Book of Acts Teach Us?

So, how do leaders navigate change? How do clergy and lay leaders navigate change? How do congregations and denominations navigate change?

May we tread on this ground—this holy ground, the sacred scriptures and the intimate lives of followers of Jesus who come to us as their shepherds—by taking off our shoes.

On the subject of human sexuality, about which there is so much brokenness in this world, there is room for repentance and humility all around. If you have come to know a gay or lesbian person who is a disciple of Jesus, you will learn again the revelation that was given to Peter in Acts 15:11: "We believe that we and they are saved in the same way, by the grace of the Lord Jesus" (CEB).

May we take off our shoes to discover what is there: Christ alone. He alone is the solid rock upon which we stand. All other ground—partisan politics, the right side of history, the mystery of human sexuality, human definitions of purity and righteousness, even the divisions within our fellowship—is sinking sand. And even more boldly, may we move forward, together, as leaders in the apostolic movement, and be able to say about our shared ministries, ones that are increasingly diverse, that "it seemed good to the Holy Spirit and to us."

GOD HATH BID ALL HUMANKIND

Romans 5

Generous Orthodoxy as Life in the Spirit

I was drawn to The United Methodist Church because of its deep, inclusive, and lifelong emphasis on the grace of God. In this tradition I came to know, trust, and worship the triune God—Father, Son, and Holy Spirit—revealed in the scriptures. In my reading and rereading of the Bible, I encountered an affirmation, which recurs six times, about the nature of God: "The Lord is compassionate and merciful, very patient, and full of faithful love" (CEB Pss 86:15, 103:8, 145:8; Exod 34:6; Neh 9:17; Joel 2:13). The nature of God is not fully defined by grace—there is, to be sure, justice and judgment—but these are attributes of God that we humans approximate, at our best, with humility. At our best, we err on the side of grace. This might even be understood as a positive expression of our first general rule, to "do no harm."

During the service of consecration, a bishop promises to uphold the unity, faith, discipline, and mission of the church. Undergirding each of these promises is the grace of God, which we experience through Jesus Christ (Rom 5; Eph 2). Again, the church at its best is nourished and sustained by the grace of God. In our doctrine, we seek to explain and give an account for the meaning and implications of this grace. It is important that we be orthodox (meaning that we believe truthfully or rightly). Yet, John Wesley was clear that believing right doctrines is not sufficient; faith is also an inward disposition of trust (expressed through his Aldersgate experience), and faith is demonstrated through acts of love (Gal 5). This synergy of belief and trust, grace and faith is at the core of our identity as United Methodist Christians. It is best captured, for me, in a phrase: generous orthodoxy.

In chapter one, we observed that an orthodox Christian holds right convictions that guide *our* thinking and believing. To be generous is to hold these same convictions with a grace and lightness that allows for flourishing and inclusion of others. The life-giving side of orthodoxy is beauty and truthfulness. The dark side of orthodoxy is the temptation to include some and to exclude others in the life of the church. A generous orthodoxy allows space for the movement of the Holy Spirit to offer the gifts of both order and freedom. In chapter four, this was the church's discernment from Acts 15 in relation to the circumcision of the Gentiles.

---- **+** ----

The Spirit's Guidance

Life in the Spirit is precisely life in the one body of Christ, wherein there is no room at the center for "I" or "we," but he is in all. In the building up of the common life of the body there will be the need for the due operation of the principles of both order and of freedom. Where these clash with one another there will be room for honest difference of opinion, and there will be need for a common seeking of the Spirit's guidance. But the mark of the person in Christ will be that he is more eager to claim freedom for his brother than for himself, and more ready to submit herself to good order than to impose it on her sister.[1]

—Lesslie Newbigin, *The Household of God*

Generous orthodoxy is made visible in United Methodism in our practice of open communion. In Luke 15, we are told that Jesus "eats with sinners," a phrase included in our liturgy of Holy Communion, and this is the impetus for his three parables about a lost sheep, a lost coin, and a lost son (or a "merciful father"). Holy Communion, like the meals that Jesus shared throughout the Gospels, is not reserved for those who perceive themselves to be righteous. Holy Communion, as a sacrament, is an outward and visible sign of the grace, or unmerited favor, of God toward all people.

The Culture Wars and Our Theological Task

I am a United Methodist because of our deep, inclusive, and lifelong doctrine of the grace of God. And over the past few years I have had the growing sense that this doctrine is a neglected resource in our silence and impasse around mission with gay and lesbian persons. Further, I am convinced that the topic of gay and lesbian participation in the church is more a matter of grace than of justice or judgment. Those on the political left often frame the question as a matter of justice, and those on the political right as a matter of judgment. A generous orthodoxy begins with God—and more specifically with God's grace.

One reason for our silence and impasse around mission with gay and lesbian people is the pervasive context of "culture wars." Strong advocacy groups press both sides of this issue, which has legal, political, and cultural implications. In the culture wars, there are winners and losers—quite literally, there are casualties—and there is at times a moral rationalization that the end (gaining political or legal advantage) justifies the means. The church often finds itself in alliances with advocacy groups on either side of the gay/lesbian question, and some congregations are identified with movements for more or less inclusion. Some want to be more open, others want to stand their ground; each senses that it is doing so out of deep Christian conviction, and each perceives itself to be countercultural.

In reflecting on this matter, my prayer is that I do not participate in or contribute to the escalation of culture wars. Given the political landscape, I am not naive in believing that it will not be heard in such a way. The polarization across the church is so pronounced that agendas are assumed. But this is not my intention. My calling is to frame the question of our mission with gay and lesbian Christians from a generously orthodox perspective, which will help us in our pastoral relationships and mission. And to do so is to find a way to navigate the culture wars.

———————— ✚ ————————

How Do We Channel Our Energies?

The conversation about LGBTQ identity and the unity of the church in the United States often occurs within the larger context of our "culture wars." I must confess that our exhaustion is due to the battle we do with each other. And yet, at the same time, there is great human suffering and injustice. In the aftermath of Hurricane Maria, many in Puerto Rico are dying. African-American youth are being profiled and killed. Young girls are trafficked. Women are harassed and abused. Too many men of color are on death row. We do not value the sacredness of the unborn. We allow the working poor to live with the risk of no healthcare. And we treat the environment as if it is a disposable commodity.

We need to channel our energies and passions toward a consistent ethic of life, for the common good. Then, perhaps, parts of our culture will know we are Christians by our love.

———————————————————

I am not arguing a dogmatic position in this chapter; rather, I am seeking to fulfill the promise I made to guard the faith, maintain the unity, and support the mission of the church. The teaching office of a bishop holds together an exposition of scripture and tradition, a vision for the church and the fulfillment of its mission, and a prophetic commitment for the alleviation of human suffering (BOD ¶403). Taken together, these activities are directly related to a bishops' "passion for the unity of the church" (BOD

¶403.e). No topic is more relevant to the unity or disunity of the church than this one.

In this chapter, I do not directly take up matters of marriage (BOD ¶161.f) or ordination (BOD ¶304), which are important subjects and are at present clearly articulated in courts of law and in the United Methodist *Discipline*, respectively. A part of the ongoing confusion related to marriage and ordination is the distinction between the church's language of gifts (in its liturgies) and the civil society's definition of rights (in its legal codes). Meanwhile, doctrine and discipline evolve in a living relationship between "Our Doctrinal Standards" (BOD ¶104) and "Our Theological Task" (BOD ¶105). So I aim to help the church have a more constructive conversation, guided by the Holy Spirit.

> Doctrine reflects the grasp of the church; theology reflects the reach of the church. To use another analogy: doctrine is the part of the cathedral already completed, exploratory theology is creative architectural vision and preliminary drawings for possible new construction.[2]

Grace Will Lead Us Home

A generous orthodoxy reclaims a deep, inclusive, and lifelong doctrine of grace, which is, for us, the way of salvation—both individually and as a church. Again, to rehearse our understanding of the movement of God's grace:

Prevenient grace is the presence of God in all people, prior to our acceptance of faith or response to divine revelation. We believe that every person is created in God's image, that all persons are of "sacred worth," and surely this is common ground, in the Wesleyan tradition, for ministries with all people. Our doctrine of prevenient grace is the basis for the conviction that no one is outside of God's love and God's saving activity.

Justifying grace is the gift of salvation, which is ours through faith and apart from any merit. The ground is indeed level at the foot of the cross. We are saved by God's grace because of faith. This salvation is God's gift. It's not something we possessed. It's not something we did that we can be proud of (Eph 2). The assurance that we can trust in the faithfulness of Jesus to save us from sin (Rom 5) was a strong emphasis in the Reformed tradition (which led to the English phrase "justified by faith") that flowed into our Wesleyan heritage.

Sanctifying grace is the journey toward holiness, and it is our lifelong response to this grace. Here our divisions become evident. Many of those who emphasize personal holiness cannot accept same-gender sexuality as a behavior in the journey to becoming more Christlike. Others who value an intentional personal relationship with Christ regard committed same-gender relationships as expressions of faithfulness. While there is no positive warrant for same-gender relationships in scripture, many interpret these relationships constructively within Jesus's commandments about love. Or they perceive prohibition against same-gender sexual intimacy as culturally conditioned teachings similar to those around slavery or polygamy or the role of women in the church.

As United Methodists, we have different interpretations of scripture, and this is related to the value we also place on reason and experience. Social justice sees the desire for inclusion as a historical movement, wedded to the struggle for civil rights and the dignity of personhood. The traditions of social justice are deeply embedded in Methodism, from our early opposition to slavery to present-day efforts to eradicate malaria.

The Simplicity and Complexity of Holiness

As we approach matters of sanctification, perfection, and holiness, our judgments should be measured by an appropriate humility, or "fear of the Lord" (a biblical acknowledgement that wisdom comes from God). The closer we come in our approach to the throne of grace, the more we become aware of our imperfections. This is a word of caution for persons who may view our understanding of LGBTQ identity in diametrically opposing ways.

The pursuit of holiness can bring out the worst and the best in us. At our worst, the pursuit of holiness can breed judgmental arrogance toward our brother or sister: "He does not believe in the authority of scripture," or "She is intolerant." The Gospels, especially the Sermon on the Mount (Matt 5–7) are clear in cautioning us about our judgments toward others. At our best, the pursuit of holiness immerses us in the love of God, which by intention flows into a love for our neighbor (1 John 4). In the Wesleyan tradition, sanctification has always been understood in practice as love of God and love of neighbor, the two great commandments of Jesus (Mark 12).

It is also true that the division of personal holiness and social justice is an artificial construct that expresses the political captivity of the church, and this division reveals the brokenness of Christ's body. To move beyond this polarization is to hear the command of the Apostle Paul: "Don't be conformed to the patterns of this world, but be transformed by the renewing of your minds so that you can figure out what God's will is—what is good and pleasing and mature" (Rom 12:2 CEB).

Exclusion as an Obstacle to Mission

Setting aside the dramatic interruptions at each of the last several United Methodist General Conferences, which have served only to harden the divisions in an increasingly global church, a steady and persistent change is occurring, accompanied by prayer, conversations within families and in congregations, and reverse-mentoring across generations.

This change is happening at the grassroots level, as local churches in the United States acknowledge the gifts of their own members and the mission field of those who are gay and lesbian, as well as their families and friends, who feel excluded by the institutional church. Some of this sense of exclusion resides in the present language of the *Book of Discipline* (BOD ¶161.f); some of it arises from negative experiences with religion; and some is the relentless stereotyping of American Christianity by a popular and secular media that cannot comprehend or communicate complexity around human sexuality and the church.

Many gay and lesbian Christians find fulfillment in their journeys as disciples of Jesus Christ in evangelical and progressive churches. At the same time, they often wonder why one particular lifestyle or issue or orientation is singled out for judgment; this present reality is surely not justified by the biblical attention given to homosexuality (in comparison, for example, to divorce and remarriage, or economic justice and poverty). This singular judgment is especially problematic for younger generations and has been documented in recent research by evangelical and progressive scholars.

The Future of The United Methodist Church

Movement on the subject of people who are gay and lesbian in The United Methodist Church is shaped by our polity, particularly our process of revising the *Book of Discipline* every four years. Our present statement includes affirmation of gay and lesbian persons, a challenge to be in ministry with them and not to condemn them, and a statement that the practice of homosexuality is incompatible with Christian teaching (BOD ¶161.f). These ambiguities reflect the sense of where our church is, at the moment, and in this regard the church reflects the culture. Indeed, it reflects the ambiguity within many individuals.

A very good statement by pastors Adam Hamilton and Mike Slaughter asked The United Methodist Church to acknowledge the varying interpretations of scripture related to people who are gay and lesbian within our denomination.[3] This amendment to the *Book of Discipline* was not accepted, even as it received significant support (47 percent) in the 2012 General Conference. At the time as a clergy leader in one of the delegations, my sense was that it was a true statement of our present reality. Given the low degree of trust, the polarization across the global church, and the ongoing and dramatic disruptions at General Conferences (by delegates, United Methodist observers, and advocates from outside the church), we were simply unable to speak the truth with each other.

I have also sensed, in the debate on homosexuality over several General Conferences, an incoherent understanding of the Way of Salvation: one argument is based upon prevenient grace and social justice, the other on repentance and justifying grace. There is little or no common ground, and thus the two groups are talking past each other. At a denominational level, there is deep suspicion and cynicism on each side about the other. In the past, some of the theological arguments for full inclusion of gay and lesbian people in the church have been less than orthodox; at the same time, many gay and lesbian Christians have responded to the grace of God, but have sensed a limited access to the means of grace. Ironically, many local churches have discovered ways to live graciously and faithfully, moving beyond the debate of abstract issues to the practices of support and accountability, or "watching over one another in love."

So, where do we go from here as a denomination? Our increasingly global church will certainly continue to shape our polity, even as sexual practices in other regions of the world, which are not affirmed by the *Book of Discipline*, go unexamined. At each successive General Conference since 2004, we have witnessed an increase in voting membership among our brothers and sisters beyond the United States. Gathering as a global church, which is a gift, has the unintended consequence of masking the decline of United Methodism in the United States. If we cannot rediscover the priority of making disciples of Jesus Christ for the transformation of the world (BOD ¶120) and learn from teaching churches that are doing just this, we will not have the capacity to fulfill God's mission, and the culture will cease to care about our positions on issues that are important to us. And, of course, this will be a central focus in the General Conferences of 2019 and 2020.

Politics and Polity

In our denominational discernment around issues related to human sexuality, we would do well not to replicate the recent experience of other denominations in the United States. In each case, the result has been schism, with devastating legal and financial consequences and diminished resources for mission. It also seems clear that movement toward a more particular political stance regarding human sexuality will not necessarily strengthen our denomination. Over the past ten years, evangelical, conservative, nondenominational, and progressive churches in the United States have all experienced decline in worship attendance.

Disagreement on the issue of human sexuality is not more difficult than other controversies with the church. Divisions have been present in Christianity since the writings of the Apostle Paul to the churches in Corinth, Galatia, and Philippi in the first century. We have resources inherent in the Methodist tradition[4]— our deep, inclusive, and lifelong doctrine of grace, our practice of open communion, our connectionalism, and our way of seeing issues missionally rather than ideologically—that can help us to navigate the future, if we allow these strengths to shape our thinking, praying, and living. In our silence, we are not bearing witness to the gifts God has given to the people called Methodist.

Some of the change, in terms of polity, will happen generationally as the demographics turn over. And yet polity will not be our salvation. Repentance, confession, forgiveness, and the journey to holiness happen in congregations and campus ministries, in small groups, Sunday school classes, and circles of trust, in the sacraments that reveal God's unmerited grace in our most ordinary experience, and in sermons that remind us that sexual orientation is not our fundamental identity. Richard Hays observes that "never within the canonical perspective (of scripture) does sexuality become the basis for defining a person's identity or for finding meaning and fulfillment in life. The things that matter are justice, mercy, and faith (Matt 23:23)."[5]

Deeper still, we are created in the image of a God who loves us, who seeks to restore the image of love in each of us, an image that is disfigured by sin—and we could name these as the sins of intolerance and sexual immorality, both of which can be expressed by the political left and right, and by gay and straight persons. The deep, inclusive, and lifelong work of grace accomplishes more than our acceptance of each other, which is not an end in itself. We are on a journey toward maturity, holiness, perfect love, and nothing less than communion with God and therefore with each other.

Good News for People Who Are Gay and Lesbian

For the sake of God's mission, I hope we will hear more clearly, and practice more faithfully, and in risk-taking ways, the statement in our *Book of Discipline*: "We implore families and churches not to reject or condemn lesbian and gay members and friends" (BOD ¶161.f), but to be in ministry for and with all persons. My hope is grounded not only in the *Discipline*, which I have promised to uphold, but in the Gospels, where, again and again, Jesus crosses boundaries to share table fellowship with outcasts.

Many gay and lesbian Christians perceive themselves to be cast out by the very churches that have formed them spiritually. The "incompatibility" sentence in the *Discipline* (BOD ¶161.f), as it reads, singles out one behavior to the exclusion of many others and contributes to this distancing, and many United Methodists simply do not know how to articulate the sentence's meaning or purpose. The result of this sentence's inclusion in our *Discipline* is an erosion in the church's teaching authority, not unlike the Roman Catholic Church's statements on contraception. Upon self-examination, we all live in ways that are "incompatible with Christian teaching" (Rom 3). This is our human condition, not the designation of one particular group of people, and is the occasion for the gift of God's grace. A generous orthodoxy would not single out a particular group for condemnation, nor would it omit a path toward restoration and reconciliation. At present, our resulting silence and impasse is not being used by God to convey the fullness of grace and truth.

A generous orthodoxy will rediscover the practices of Jesus in the Gospels, calling all people into communion with him. Is that call a tacit approval of who we are, in our humanity? No, and this is true for gay and straight people. Again, the ground is indeed level at the foot of the cross, and this is the common ground of grace. This grace inspired a movement in eighteenth-century England and nineteenth-century America that made disciples who in turn transformed the world. But more fundamentally, this grace was invitational and evangelical.

I am convinced that God is calling us, in the twenty-first century, to share the gospel, in less harmful words and through more gracious actions, with all people, and surely among them are our gay and lesbian neighbors. I am also convinced that welcoming people who are gay and lesbian will open us more fully to their gifts, among them testimonies of courage and patience, faith and grace. And I am equally persuaded that these callings flow from a clear and generously orthodox Christian faith, grounded in scripture and our tradition.

We are saved by God's grace; this is true for straight and gay people, for individuals and for a denomination. Our future mission is not one of condemnation but of invitation:

> Come, sinners to the gospel feast
> Let every soul be Jesus' guest.
> You need not one be left behind
> For God hath bid all humankind.
>   (Charles Wesley)

Chapter Six

A CATHOLIC SPIRIT RECONSIDERED

Matthew 13

W hile serving as pastor of congregations for twenty-eight years, I would occasionally notice the absence of a formerly active parishioner, and a thought would cross my mind: I wonder where that family has been lately? I would then encounter her at the athletic field, or him in a grocery store, and we would begin an inevitably awkward conversation. There would be an embarrassing pause, and then a brief conversation. "We've decided to find another church," they would tell me. And then the reasons for leaving would unfold: a contentious relationship, an unpopular social position, an unmet expectation in worship, a judgment—harsh or restrained—about someone's morality.

In a culture that teaches us to self-identify according to real or perceived desires, I understood. And yet, as a pastor, I always hoped for a deeper relationship that could be grounded in something more than preference. Now, as a bishop, this drama is repeated on a larger stage. The situation involves the expectations of clergy and laity, movements and obstacles related to justice, and the desire to be unshackled from institutions, even as those same institutions supply the resources we want, need, and have come to expect.

Robert Putnam's book *Bowling Alone* explains our need for community, and Robert Bellah's *Habits of the Heart* identifies the powerful forces that undermine it. I have experienced the joy of unity and the beauty of diversity. And I have known their painful absence.

So, what motivates us to live in community? And what might inspire us to stay in community, or remain as one denomination, as The United Methodist Church, alongside those who hold starkly different positions than us on matters that are of such great importance?

A helpful source for us, as followers of Jesus, is his parable of the wheat and the weeds (Matt 13:24-30). We sometimes yearn for a vineyard that would be more holy, just, or pure if those with whom we have conflict are no longer present. There was evidently a temptation in the Jewish culture, at the same time the early church emerged, to define communal discipline by weeding out "followers of the evil one." In Jesus's teaching, we are urged not to undertake any kind of weeding out or uprooting. This is finally and in time the work of God. In the vivid image of Jesus's parable, we grow together, wheat and weeds, in the church. This is a call to live together, patiently aware of our own imperfections and those of others. At times we live together in the midst of an experience that is moderately discomforting; and at other times, our relationships are strained by matters that go to the core or who we are and who we aspire to be.

In our denomination, the most divisive matter is the conversation around human sexuality, which is at times framed as an "issue" and more often lived in family and parish relationships. I insist here that we not characterize the straight person as the wheat and the gay and lesbian person as the weed, or progressives as the wheat and conservatives as the weeds! Nobel Laureate Alexandr Solzhenitsyn observed, "The line separating good and evil passes not through states, nor between classes, nor between political parties either, but right through every human heart."

To say that the wheat and the weeds grow within each of us is to acknowledge our acceptance of grace and our need for confession. The warning about removing the weeds from the wheat is not to become passive or complacent. Rather, in removing the weeds, we will also uproot the wheat. How does one speak out of conviction about one aspect of a person's life without doing harm to themselves or to a family? None of us is one-dimensional, and none of us can be reduced to any issue! If we can be reduced to any common experience, it is surely our need for the grace of God.

To add complexity, the seed (God's word) speaks differently to each of us, and the shallowness of a local church's soil can be a function of the desire to be relevant or the steady stream of messages in the social media that distort the still, small Voice. Most leaders in our denomination would agree that we are not in a place that positions us for the substantive conversation that is so often needed. Contributing factors to this environmental condition are the lack of deep spiritual formation in many congregations, inadequate theological formation of youth and their parents, weakening denominational infrastructures (support for camps, campus ministries, church-related colleges and theological schools), a market economy whose mobility diminishes long-term, trust-filled relationships, and a surrounding culture that is increasingly secular, materialistic, and individualistic.

The difficulty in having a mature conversation around issues of human sexuality (or racial profiling or "stand your ground" laws or immigration) is shaped in part by the shallowness of our spirituality, the weakness of our congregational life, and the fragmentation of our communities, and now, it seems, our denomination.

And so we are tempted to flee from those who challenge us. The "homogeneous unit principle," which deserved criticism among the church-growth consultants, turns out to define us when we simply want to hang out with people who think, vote, pray, and behave like us. This may not be a conscious decision. It simply requires less energy to stay in our own small tribes!

---------------- ✚ ----------------

No Winners or Losers

In my tribe there are no winners or losers, only actions and reactions. And in my tribe, there are deeply divergent conceptions of grace and holiness. This is the work to be done. The question is, can we do as little harm to each other as possible so that we might do this work together, not to change the mind of the other, but to see Christ in them, even as we wish that others would see our Lord in us?

The presenting issue is political, and in some ways it is easier to keep it there. The theological and spiritual effort is harder, and requires more of us, because God is never finished with us and is always calling us back into community. As Thomas Merton said in *The Sign of Jonas*, "By making a vow of stability the monk renounces the vain hope of wandering off to find the perfect monastery. This implies a deep act of faith; the recognition that it does not much matter where we are." In community, he insisted, we above all love one another as Christ has loved us.[1]

Perhaps we hope for something more. And yes, perhaps the Gospels call us toward the creation of something better. So we live together, wheat and weeds. The church is never a static institution. It is always changing. At its best, the church is a kind of "greenhouse" where we are planted, cultivated, pruned, and thus transformed. To live together is a gift of grace, to remain in a real church in a local context, and not in Dietrich Bonhoeffer's description of the community that is our "wish dream."[2] It is to participate in the means of grace with other sinners who are also invited to the gospel feast. This is an essential activity in our maturing as disciples until the harvest where God is both a gracious and just redeemer. So we discern, judge, and evaluate; but, as Reinhold Niebuhr wrote in a sermon on this parable, "while we have to judge, there is a judgment beyond our judgment, and there are fulfillments beyond our fulfillments."[3]

The practices of humility and patience, from a human point of view, can seem somewhat passive and even indifferent, particularly when the energies that flow toward opposing convictions threaten to fracture the community. And yet we trust in the slow and steady shaping of providence, we hope for what we do not see, and we "grow side by side until the harvest" (Matt 13:30).

---✛---

It Happens

If you are a member of a denomination of several million people, it is likely that someone at some point in time will say or do something that will be offensive to you. It happens. Be at peace.

I would encourage Christians who cannot accept gay and lesbian persons, in orientation or practice, to place the judgment of them (and all of us) in God's hands. As the Apostle Paul asks, "Who is in a position to condemn?" (Rom 8). And I would encourage gay and lesbian Christians to be patient with their brothers and sisters in the church who have not walked their journey. This is not a justification for continued injustice. And yet it is also true that sexuality itself is a mysterious, complicated, and emotionally charged subject. Rational conversation and dialogue will emerge only if those who disagree come to the table hearing the admonition of James: "Everyone should be quick to listen, slow to speak, and slow to grow angry" (Jas 1:19). I am encouraged that some are seeking to recover the model of E. Stanley Jones's roundtable in India, which held the conviction that "God is trying to speak to us, and God will use all of us to construct that message."

Patience is here understood not as a false tolerance of difference. I am speaking of the patience of God toward us, and the calling we have, as disciples of Jesus Christ, to more fully reveal the image of God to each other. Such patience is the fruit of the Spirit (Gal 5) in families and in congregations across our denomination. This patience is an essential mark of our mission with people who are gay and lesbian, which itself is grounded in generous orthodoxy. Patience resides in our participation in the lifelong experience of grace, which is the power of God to transform us.

In the Gospels, a vivid portrait of patience is found in Jesus's parable of the wheat and the tares (Matt 13). We are sometimes tempted to see the vineyard as more holy or just if those with whom we have conflict are no longer present. In the beautiful image of Jesus's parable, we grow together, wheat and tares, in the church. In this way, the church is a "greenhouse" where we are planted, pruned (John 15), and thus transformed. To live together (even in our differences) is a gift of grace, and is essential in our maturing as disciples, until the harvest where God is the judge.

> Christians experience growth and transition in their spiritual life just as in their physical and emotional lives. While this growth is always a work of grace, it does not occur uniformly. Spiritual growth in Christ is a dynamic process marked by awakening, birth, growth, and maturation. This process requires careful and intentional nurture for the disciple to reach perfection in the Christian life.[4]

As Methodists, we have understood this to be our way of life, with God and with each other. In "The Character of a Methodist," John Wesley commented that "as to all opinions that do not strike at the root of Christianity, we think and let think."[5] And in "A Plain Account of Christian Perfection," he insists that "orthodoxy, or right opinions, is at best a slender part of religion, if it can be allowed to be any part at all." His sermon on the "Catholic Spirit" is focused around a question and an answer taken from 2 Kings 10:15: "Is your heart right with my heart? If it is, then give me your hand." His interpretation of this verse of scripture is worthy of our reflection:

> "If it is, give me your hand." I do not mean, "Be of my opinion." You need not. I do not expect or desire it. Neither do I mean, "I will be of your opinion." I cannot; it does not depend on my choice. I can no more think than I can see or hear as I will. Keep you your opinion; I mine, and that as steady as ever. You need not endeavour to come over to me or bring me over to you. I do not desire to dispute those points or to hear or speak one word concerning them. Let all opinions alone on one side and the other: only, "give me your hand."[6]

He likens the catholic spirit to the universal spirit or universal love, and concludes, "lastly, love me not in word only but in deed and in truth. So far as in conscience you can (retaining still your own opinions and your own manner of worshipping God), join with me in the work of God, and let us go on hand in hand." In the language of the Wesleyan tradition, a generous orthodoxy toward God is expressed through a catholic spirit toward each other, for the sake of our common mission in the world. And this results in a call to fruitfulness:

Join with me in the work of God!

In 1999, Thomas Langford addressed the United Methodist Council of Bishops in a lecture entitled "Grace Upon Grace." His theological exploration led, in the end, to the question of homosexuality. He spoke of a grace that is "the reach of God even to those who are alienated from God," interpreting the hymn "Love Divine, All Loves Excelling" (Jesus, Thou art all compassion!) and 1 Corinthians 13 (grace bears, believes, hopes, endures all things, and grace never fails). He then concluded with a dialogue between this grace and the issue of homosexuality and same-gender marriage.

He cautioned us to begin with humility, noting that each side of the debate "often claim the moral high ground." He then invited us to "quiet down, recognize the awesomeness of God's grace and be humble." This humility grants us the time and space to seek God's will, which is imperative for a matter with such complexity. He writes,

> The issue is so complex that it cannot be quickly resolved. Perhaps United Methodism can become the exception and await the guidance of God. It may be that in the end we shall not reach consensus. It may be that we shall not be held together in the Body of Christ by agreement, but by love.[7]

And then he notes that there is precedence for such a time of waiting, praying, and being in relationship with one another. He mentions other moral issues on which Christians do not agree, among them war, divorce, and abortion.[8] He then concludes,

> If we can stay together, it may be only with tension and disagreement over the nature and implications of homosexuality to separate the Body of Christ. If we can stay together, it may be only with tension and disagreement, but until we know more and understand the will of God better, we may by grace have to learn to live with fellow Christians who disagree with us.

So we grow together, the wheat and the weeds. Every now and then, whether in the first century or in the twenty-first century, there is an impulse to uproot and purify the community, to surround ourselves with those who resemble our own vision of where God is leading us. It is a natural human impulse. Jesus must have sensed it in his own community, and so he gave the disciples and us this parable.

Let the weeds grow a little higher, Jesus says to us. It makes no sense, in morality or in agriculture, and yet, in the kingdom of God, it is the higher way. "In uprooting the weeds you will do harm to the wheat. In destroying what you perceive to be evil in your neighbor, you will do harm to the community and to yourself."

So, what might motivate us or inspire us to live in community? I think this is precisely why Jesus taught this parable, why John Wesley reflected on the "Catholic Spirit," why Thomas Langford struggled with the Council of Bishops fifteen years ago in his lecture, why the question emerges in these days.

There is no grand answer, but there is guidance for us: We let the weeds grow a little higher, trusting in the providence of God.

We let the weeds grow a little higher, remembering that the Lord is our judge.

---+---

Judgment

Final judgment belongs to God, and we have to beware of judging before the time. I think that if we refuse fellowship in Christ to any body of men and women who accept Jesus as Lord and show the fruits of His Spirit in their corporate life, we do so at our peril. With what judgment we judge we shall be judged. It behooves us therefore to receive one another as Christ has received us.[9]

We let the weeds grow a little higher, grateful for the patience of the One who has begun a good work in us, and, the scripture promises, will be faithful to complete it (Phil 1:6).

WE DO NOT LOSE HEART

2 Corinthians 5

First Be Reconciled

We live in a deeply divided time. This is reflective of our recent presidential election in the United States, but it is also true for nations across our global church, in Africa and Europe and the Philippines. And the divisions are real in our own denomination. The Commission on a Way Forward was called into being by the General Conference in 2016 to look for the missional purposes that might transcend the many matters that divide us, ones rooted not only in understandings of LGBTQ identity but in the interpretation of scripture and the nature and mission of the church.

The question before us is, what do these divisions mean for disciples of Jesus Christ in the Wesleyan tradition? And, more purposefully, how can we be disciples of Jesus Christ who are transforming the world in the context of so much division? The Commission on a Way Forward is but one of the instruments

God is using to answer this question. But the work of reconciliation happens in nations, in communities, in congregations, in families and relationships, and within each of us.

What are the practices that lead to reconciliation? And how does the gospel shape such practices?

The gospel is at the core of our faith, and the Sermon on the Mount is at the core of the gospel. Of the forty-four Standard Sermons of John Wesley, thirteen were based on the Sermon on the Mount. The sermon begins with the Beatitudes: how life is blessed, how we flourish, what happiness means. Upon reading these first few verses of Matthew 5, we see a reversal of the world's values. Disciples of Jesus are the salt of the earth and the light of the world. There is something different, distinctive about being a follower of Jesus. Southern writer Flannery O'Connor commented, "You shall know the truth and the truth shall make you odd!"

Then, in a statement to encourage Jewish followers, Jesus said he has not come to abolish the Hebrew Bible—this is not "out with the old, in with the new!"—but he has come to fulfill the law and the prophets. And then he gives the six antitheses—"you have heard it said, but I say to you." Jesus is giving us a model for a higher righteousness.

He begins with murder, violence, and anger. Jesus has a way of taking a subject that seems to apply to other people, other groups, and bringing it close to home. He has quit preaching and gone to meddling! All of a sudden, when we are in the presence of Jesus, the distrust, the suspicion, the anger is within us. In the best of families, in the best of churches, there is conflict. And in the best of families, in the best of churches, there is a need for reconciliation.

So back to our question: What practices might lead to reconciliation? Before you place your gift on the altar, Jesus says to first be reconciled to your brother or sister (Matt 5:23). Turn the other cheek. Go the extra mile. Love your enemies. We often want to be in relationship. And we usually want to be right. Herein lies the tension: it is more important to be in a right relationship than to be right. We sometimes neglect this truth. The addictive nature of the culture wars pulls us apart, or the impulse within us to win ("what's in it for my group?") causes the divisions to become more and more pronounced.

Revival as Reconciliation

Early in ministry I served a rural, four-point charge, which is four churches that share a pastor and live in harmony. Or something like that.

Well, every fall and spring each church would have revival services that would last several days. This meant I had eight weeks of revival a year. I was a very revived person!

The stated purpose of these revival services was to reach and save the lost. They began on Sunday morning, and they continued on Sunday evening through Wednesday or Thursday evening. And so I would be listening to the visiting preacher on or about Wednesday evening, and the message would be about the lost and how they and we needed to be found, and I would look out at the congregation and think, "These people are not lost. They are the committed core!" After all, they are here on the third or fourth night!

And I wondered, "Why do we have all of these services? What is the purpose?" And then, in time, it was as if God spoke to me and gave me an answer.

When you live in a small community, no one new ever moves in or moves out. You go to school together, you do business with each other, families blend together, things happen. We do harm to each other. Other people do harm to us. They do harm to people we love. If you live long enough, it happens. Even in the best of families.

And we begin to construct walls. Right down the middle between us. And here is where the revival services came in. What was happening in those services was that we were being called to make things right with each other. And so people would come forward and they would kneel at the altar and they would make peace with their Creator and they would make peace with someone—a neighbor, family member, a business partner—and they would leave it there at the altar. It was reconciliation.

What would it mean in a culture and, yes, in a church divided in most every way, for us to first be reconciled, to turn the other cheek, to follow the example of these mature disciples, to go the extra mile, to love our enemies?

———————————— ✛ ————————————

There is something deeply Wesleyan about this teaching of Jesus in the Sermon on the Mount. I cannot be holy without you, and you cannot be holy without me. This is the connectional nature of our church. This is social holiness. As Andrew Thompson observed, Wesley does not bifurcate holiness (as in personal holiness and social holiness). Said differently, social holiness is not a synonym for social justice. There is no holiness but social holiness, Wesley insisted. My relationship with my neighbor has everything to do with the sacrifice, the gift I am offering to God. This is the wholeness we seek. It is the integration we need in our minds and our bodies and spirits, in our communities and in our state and nation and world.

We are not there yet. That is why we need Jesus.

First be reconciled, Jesus says.

The Altar, Again

I had the privilege of meeting with several members of the Emanuel African Methodist Episcopal Church in Charleston, South Carolina. Commonly referred to as "Mother Emanuel," this AME Church came into being when Richard Allen, an African American, was asked to leave the Methodist Church in Philadelphia in 1787. Richard Allen was later ordained by Francis Asbury in 1799 and consecrated a bishop by Asbury in 1816.

Emanuel Church was planted in Charleston during this time. It is the oldest black church of any kind in the southern region of the United States. In 1822, it was burned to the ground because it had become a center of teaching and preaching about liberation and freedom among slaves. It was then rebuilt and still is a vital church today.

In 2015, a young man drove two hours to Charleston, went into the church on a Wednesday night, and took part in the Bible study. At the conclusion of the Bible study, everyone stood and closed their eyes in prayer. In the next few seconds, the young man fired seventy-four bullets from a semi-automatic weapon, killing nine people, including the pastor.[1]

We listened to their story, and at the end we all walked to the altar. At the time I tried to imagine the grief of the people who worship there. I have since wondered: What is God calling me to do, to understand how I need to be a part of the solution to the pain and the injustice and the unrighteousness? First, be reconciled, Jesus says. Turn the other cheek. Go the extra mile. Love your enemies.

Jesus is teaching what he will come to embody. "So we are ambassadors who represent Christ. God is negotiating with you through us. We beg you as Christ's representatives, 'Be reconciled to God!'" This is the end of 2 Corinthians 5. And then Paul continues, in the next chapter:

> Since we work together with him, we are also begging you not to receive the grace of God in vain. He says, *I listened to you at the right time, and I helped you on the day of salvation.* Look, now is the right time! Look, now is the day of salvation! (2 Cor 6:1-2)

Our salvation, as Wesleyans, is completed in holiness, what Wesley called Christian perfection. Jesus says in his sermon, "In showing love to everyone, so also you must be complete" (Matt 5:48 CEB). In the KJV language of Wesley's day, "Be ye therefore perfect, even as your heavenly Father which in heaven is perfect." In Luke's Gospel, the parallel phrase from the sermon is "Be merciful, as your Father is merciful." The early church heard Jesus saying these words after his instructions to first be reconciled, to turn the other cheek, to go the extra mile, to love our enemies. Be perfect in showing love. Be merciful. In his commentary on these words, New Testament scholar Ben Witherington notes that "to be perfect here means to love in the same indiscriminate way that God loves."[2]

74

Indiscriminate.

We confess that we need this teaching of Jesus, and the ongoing presence of the Holy Spirit to discern what it means for us. And perhaps in our journey to perfection we need not neglect mercy. And in our extension of mercy we can confess that we have not yet arrived at complete or perfect love. We must not allow disagreement over our understandings of LGBTQ identity to divide the church. And yet we must not seek or settle for unity at the expense of the other's dignity or sacred worth.

We Do Not Lose Heart

There is much work to be done. And along the way we may be tempted to give up, to disconnect, to despair.

I camped out for a time in 2 Corinthians 4, and this is where God led me.

1. "We are not depressed" ("do not lose heart," 2 Cor 4:16), leads to…

2. "We live by faith, not by sight" (2 Cor 5:7), leads to…

3. "We won't recognize people by human standards" (2 Cor 5:16), leads to…

4. God has reconciled us to himself through Christ (2 Cor 5:18), leads to…

5. Christ gave us the ministry of reconciliation (2 Cor 5:18).

If we are reconciling persons, (1) we do not give up, (2) we live in trust and hope, (3) we do not define people with sociological or political labels, and (4) reconciliation is something God does first in us, through the cross.

If we are willing to embrace these first four steps, then (5) God will use us in the needed ministry of reconciliation. The words for "reconciliation" and "reconcile" appear rarely in the New Testament;[3] in ordinary Greek usage the words *katalasso* and *katalagge* are not associated with religious belief or practice. Instead, the words were often employed in the realm of politics and the resolution of conflicts.[4]

The work of reconciliation was needed in Corinth. Corinth was factionalized, and the people in the fellowship challenged Paul's leadership. In Paul's response to them, he insisted that the cross put to death our ways of labeling and defining each other. In the process, they were becoming a part of God's new creation. This reconciliation was not simply about individuals; God was in Christ reconciling the world to himself.

Furthermore, God was giving to us the ministry (*diakonia*) of reconciliation. The church of Jesus Christ, in the present moment, hungers for this ministry.

Our Two-Cell Fights and a Third Way

Many of our churches are engaged in two-cell fights, to borrow the language of Kennon Callahan. Some call this "binary thinking." The two cells might be:

long-time members and newcomers

natives and transplants

the contemporary service and the traditional service

the people who liked the last pastor and the people who
   like the new pastor

Republicans and Democrats

Wesleyans and Calvinists

traditionalists and progressives

Methodists and nondenominational Christians

persons of color and Anglos

the rich and the poor

So, there is a two-cell fight. And we are given the ministry of reconciliation. Family systems psychologist Ed Friedman defined stress, at its core, as being called to negotiate a two-cell fight. The way forward, he suggested, was to grow a third cell. Start a third worship service. Form a third political party. Find a third way.

For Christians, the ultimate third way is the power of God. The revival service in that rural church was a ritual way of accessing the power of God. Revival may very well be the way The United Methodist Church experiences a breakthrough. It may be the way we become unstuck.

---------------------- ✚ ----------------------

You, the God who can save us, restore us!
  Stop being angry with us!
Will you be mad at us forever?
  Will you prolong your anger from one generation to
    the next?
Won't you bring us back to life again
  so that your people can rejoice in you?
(Psalm 85:4-7 CEB)

Psalm 85 begins with the reminder that God has done this before. There have been Great Awakenings and Pentecostal breakthroughs. In each generation, God has been doing a new thing. This is about forgiveness and pardon, transparency and assurance, and God seeing something in us that we did not always see in ourselves. This is about God restoring us to our original purpose. Revival and restoration are intertwined with loyal love, faithfulness, righteousness, and peace. These are the conditions for revival, and these are the fruit of revival. We cannot manipulate God. God is not at our disposal. But we can put ourselves in a place where we are more likely to encounter God. For John Wesley, this was the relationship between the *means* of grace and the *movement* of grace in our lives.

Revival is always a return, a remembrance of all that Jesus Christ has done for us (one has died for all), and the consequence of that is we are now in relation to one another. This relationship is grounded in the very nature of God and is more than what we often see on the surface. The "human point of view" of which Paul often speaks is embodied in our selfish desires, *kata sarx*.

How do we look at people according to the world's ways of classifying us or about our attributes, external conditions, or status in society? Are our judgments based on what is external rather than internal? Here, we confess, our human judgment is flawed by prejudice and privilege.

Could it be that the work of reconciliation changes us before it changes others?

Reconciliation is the act of exchanging the old for the new, war for peace, anger for love, estrangement for relationship. We become stuck by becoming comfortable, even complacent in the old world. Our divisions are normalized. Our prejudices become habits. Our sin takes on a familiarity.

The New Creation

The intervention of God is to initiate reconciliation through Jesus Christ and by the power of the cross. To view Christ according to our selfish desires is to empty him of the passion, death, and resurrection, to see him in his humanity but not his divinity, in his weakness but not in his victory. To see Christ according to the Spirit is to imagine the possibility of this cosmic agenda. This cosmic agenda is the new creation, which appears twice in the New Testament, in 2 Corinthians 4 and in Galatians 6:15. The latter verse reads: "Being circumcised or not being circumcised doesn't mean anything. What matters is a new creation" (Gal 6:15 CEB). It has an interesting parallel in the same letter: "Being circumcised or not being circumcised doesn't matter in Christ Jesus, but faith working through love does matter" (Gal 5:6 CEB).

This verse, and the dynamic of "faith working through love," was a favorite of John Wesley's. Paul and his interpreters are saying that a sign of the new creation is faith working through love. What is faith working through love? Paul anticipated this question earlier in Galatians—it's "the faithfulness of God's Son, who loved me and gave himself for me" (2:20). This is the initiative of God and the self-identification of God with us through the incarnation.

Once we receive the initiative that is God's, who has reconciled with us through the cross, we know by faith that we are justified, and we have peace with God (Rom 5). This peace allows us to enter into the ministry of reconciliation, and to sustain this work, even when we are tempted to lose heart.

Meditation is one of God's ways of giving us access to a new way of seeing and being in relationship. I invite you into this meditation and to expand on it in ways that are relevant to your own experience. The meditation seeks to bring the New Testament into a living dialogue with the concepts in *The Anatomy of Peace,* and the condition of a heart at war or a heart at peace.

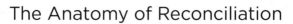

The Anatomy of Reconciliation

When we have a heart at peace, we see others as persons.
When we have a heart at war, we see others as objects.
When we see others as persons, we look for ways to help
 things go right.
When we see others as objects, we exaggerate our differences.
When we have a heart at peace, we admit that we may be a
 part of the problem.
When we have a heart at war, we see others as the problem.
When we want to create change, we build relationships.
When we want to perpetuate the status quo, we seek to fix
 or change others.

When we have a heart at peace, we practice forgiveness and
reconciliation.

When we have a heart at war, we take up the weapons of
conflict and collusion.

When we have a heart at peace, we listen to the lives of
others.

When we have a heart at war, we make assumptions about
the lives of others.

When we listen to the lives of others, we see them as
persons.

When we do not listen to the lives of others, we see them as
objects.

We honor ourselves—the image of God—when we seek
peace.

We betray ourselves—the image of God—when we go to
war.

We influence other people by building relationships.

We build relationships by listening and noticing.

When we notice, we liberate others—they become persons
and not objects.

When we listen and notice in healthy relationships,
correction is possible.

We move from peace to war in small, almost imperceptible
ways.

We move from peace to war in the choices we make.

A heart at peace develops through practices like centering
prayer.

The sacred word in centering prayer can take us into the
heart of God,

which is peace.

A heart at peace develops through the practice of silence.

In silence we notice the persons we encounter,

we hear their voices more clearly,

and we see the image of God in them.

81

A heart at peace leaves a gift at the altar,
and moves toward the brother or sister
toward whom we are estranged.
A heart at peace has a sure trust and confidence
in the One who was in Christ,
reconciling the world to himself.
And a heart at peace has the resources to enter into this
   ministry of reconciliation.

THE LOCAL OPTION, FROM CORINTH TO THE PRESENT MOMENT

1 Corinthians 12

The promise of this era, in cultural terms just as in economic terms, is the promise of diversity and choice. The danger of this era, in cultural just as is in economic terms, is the danger of polarization and division. And the work of maximizing the promise while minimizing the danger—of enabling more of our fellow citizens to live out their own American dreams without losing the essential unifying power of a commonly held American Dream—is a foremost challenge for our politics in the coming years.[1]

Yuval Levin's observation about diversity in America has an implication for The United Methodist Church. Our **promise** is to allow for as much differentiation as possible in a global and democratic church. This becomes necessary whether you exist in Monrovia, Liberia; in Birmingham, Alabama; in Portland, Oregon; or in Manila, Philippines. At a congregational level, we allow for this differentiation: a church can choose to highlight or hide the name "United Methodist"; it can baptize infants in one-parent households, perform marriages for couples where one person has been previously married, contribute to mission work that is ecumenical or nondenominational, shape worship around the lectionary or not, and the list goes on. We call this, in Levin's language, "diversity and choice." Some Methodists have pejoratively referred to this as the "local option."

✛

The Local Option

- A local church can brand itself by the cross and flame or not—this is the local option

- A local church can support United Methodist and nondenominational missionaries—this is the local option

- A local church can hire staff members who are not United Methodists—this is the local option

- United Methodist candidates for ministry can attend seminaries that are not United Methodist—this is the local option

- A local church can offer traditional and contemporary styles of worship—this is the local option

- A local church can design its own process for discipleship—this is the local option

- A local church in Monrovia, Liberia, can design outreach to its community that differs from a local church in Los Angeles, California, or Toledo, Ohio, or Miami, Florida—this is the local option

- A local church can baptize by sprinkling, pouring, or immersion—this is the local option
- Theological schools make their own decisions about whom they admit as students and which faculty receive tenure—this is the local option
- A local church can sing hymns or praise choruses, it can say the Apostles' Creed and the Lord's Prayer, or not—this is the local option

The phrase "local option" takes on a pejorative connotation among some, but underneath the criticism there is actually a healthy practice of permission-giving and contextualization. Let's be honest and say that most of us live the "local option" every day in multiple ways, and we do so to reach as many people as we can, in strategic ways, with the gospel.

The United Methodist Church will benefit in the coming years by having a better conversation about what is local, what is contextual, what serves the mission, and which is our purpose.

Our **danger** is, of course, that we become more diffuse and fragmented, less clear about purpose, increasingly unable to account for the reasons that we might continue to be united. The seeds of this are present in our differentiation *when such differentiation is not articulated in missional, pastoral, or theological ways.* Roughly half of our clergy are trained in schools and traditions outside our denomination—some free church, some pan-Wesleyan, some Reformed, some affiliated with mainline (establishment) denominations. The default rationale is often proximity and geography; but the end result is more diffusion and fragmentation.

The fragmentation may also be the result of our legislative and judicial processes, which themselves have at their core a need to describe one's own position as right/just and the other as wrong/unjust, and the resulting media coverage (within and beyond the denomination) that is binary in its form. Binary communication creates polarization and division in ecclesial and political culture.

So, how do we "maximize the promise while minimizing the danger"?

It helps to begin by stating the urgency. The work of the Council of Bishops and the Commission on a Way Forward is very clear that we are in unprecedented territory. It is unlikely that the status quo will remain in place. Of course, there is a need for change. But much good can also be lost. This was a part of my argument in my chapter in the book *Finding our Way: Love and Law in The United Methodist Church.*

It also helps to note the ways in which the church is a reflection of the larger culture. Many of the skills we have learned, ones that deconstruct, divide, and stereotype, are easily transferred from participation in culture to leadership in the church. This occurs in advocacy and renewal groups, but the Council of Bishops, General Agencies, and local churches are not immune from these behaviors.

So how do we create a different culture? Or, in Yuval Levin's language, how do we focus less attention on "dominating our core cultural institutions and more on building thriving subcultures"?[2]

"Maximizing the promise while minimizing the danger" requires the building of trust, intimacy, and respect among leaders. What would motivate us to do this work? Perhaps it is in the enabling of our fellow citizens (members and participants) to live out their own American dreams (discipleship) without losing the essential unifying power (connection) of a commonly held American Dream (a United Methodist Church).

A part of our future must be a refocusing on what it means to be a disciple, and that is in itself grounded in knowing the life and teachings of Jesus and the experience of the early church, what Wesley would have called "primitive Christianity." We cannot assume this. And so it helps to return to the ancient source, the early church, and to learn about an apostolic attempt to articulate a "thriving subculture."

The Gifts of a Divided Church

The Apostle Paul is writing in the first century to a divided church. There were divisions in the church, even in its earliest expression. In this instance, the divisions were about the gifts of speaking in tongues (*glosson, glossolalia*) and prophecy (*propheteia*). Some saw themselves as being more spiritual than others. Paul speaks into the context of the church in Corinth by using the framework of God's gifts and grace.

> There are different spiritual gifts (*charismaton*) but the same Spirit; and there are different ministries (*diakonion*) and the same Lord; and there are different activities (*energematon*), but the same God who produces all of them in everyone. (1 Cor 12:4-6 CEB)

Here Paul speaks of the relationship between gifts, service, and energy. We are in our "sweet spot" when these dynamics form a triangle. We are at our best and we are fulfilling God's purpose in our lives and our callings when we hold these three words together.

The word *gift* (*charismata*) is rooted in the word for grace, *charis*. This reminds us that any gift that we might have is a gift of God's grace, and not our achievement or merit.

Spirituality is also connected to service. Bishop Richardo Pereira of the Methodist Church of Cuba told me once of the revival in that church. Many would pray through the night to receive charismatic gifts. Once, two young men came to him and said, "We prayed all night, we have received the gift. Now what do you want us to do?" He responded, "Now that you have received the gift of the Spirit, there is a mop leaning against the wall. You could begin by cleaning the church!"

- What is your gift?

- How are you serving?

- Where is your energy?

"A demonstration of the Spirit is given to each person for the common good." (1 Cor 12:7 CEB)

The word *sympheron* comes from Greek and Roman politics, and it is related to coming together for mutual benefit. It is also a cognate of our word *symphony*. How do we hear many voices, both the louder and the more muted voices? It is clear that we are given spiritual gifts not for individual self-definition but for others. After I served in pastoral ministry for twenty-eight years and began to serve briefly as a district superintendent and then as a bishop, I realized that this work is not about us. We do this work for others. We sit at these tables in order to see the gifts of others.

> "Christ is just like the human body—a body is a unit and has many parts; and all the parts of the body are one body, even though there are many." (1 Cor 12:12 CEB)

Here Paul writes of the paradox of holding together differences amidst a common source, the one and the many. A paradox is understood as a term from Latin for two truths, side by side. I often want to see "my" truth in contrast to what is "false." How can we think in the way of the Apostle Paul, who was able to place more than one truth alongside another?

> "We were all baptized by one Spirit into one body, whether Jew or Greek, or slave or free, and we all were given one Spirit to drink." (1 Cor 12:13 CEB)

Here Paul does not add "male or female" (Gal 3:28). Why? I invite you to pursue this in your own study of the Bible!

> Indeed, the body does not consist of one member but of many. If the foot would say, "Because I am not a hand, I do not belong to the body," that would not make it any less a part of the body. And if the ear would say, "Because I am not an eye, I do not belong to the body," that would not make it any less a part of the body. If the whole body were an eye, where would the hearing be? If the whole body were hearing, where would the sense of smell be? But as it is, God arranged the members in the body, each one of them, as he chose. If all were a single member, where would the body be? As it is, there are many members, yet one body (1 Cor 12:14-20 NRSV).

The composition of the members of the body leads to its healthy functioning. To identify the body through only one of its members would be to restrict its capacity. This is the beauty of diversity.

> So the eye can't say to the hand, "I don't need you," or in turn, the head can't say to the feet, "I don't need you." Instead, the parts of the body that people think are the weakest are the most necessary. The parts of the body that we think are less honorable are the ones we honor the most. The private parts of our body that aren't presentable are the ones that are given the most dignity. The parts of our body that are presentable don't need this. But God has put the body together, giving greater honor to the part with less honor. (1 Cor 12:21-24 CEB)

Throughout this passage, Paul names the relationships between strength and weakness, being honored and despised, between superiority and inferiority, being privileged and marginalized. In a siloed and gerrymandered world, where we retreat to our own kind (I confess this as my own temptation!), the organic connection of each part of the body to another is essential. God designed us in precisely this way—to be in relationship with each other in the body of Christ.

These relationships have a profound way of shaping our life together. Richard Hays writes that "a conversion of the imagination will be necessary for those in a position of privilege truly to see themselves as bound together with the weaker members of the body."[3]

> So that there won't be division in the body and so the parts might have mutual concern for each other. If one part suffers, all the parts suffer with it; if one part gets the glory, all the parts celebrate with it. (1 Cor 12:25-26 CEB)

Paul writes to a divided church, but the divisions should not be regarded as normal or the status quo. God's design is that there be no divisions or schisms. The word *schism* is a Greek cognate to our word *scissors*—our calling is not to cut up the fabric that is the church. Schism might be described as the absence of our suffering and rejoicing together. There is no form of church that will not include suffering. As Thomas Merton notes, "the body of Christ can be described as the resetting of a body of broken bones." In the church we will suffer together. And yet this calls forth our compassion.

The writings of the New Testament did not originally include numbers for chapters and verses. These were actually added many centuries later. First Corinthians 12–14 actually form an extended teaching about divisions and spiritual gifts. At the core of this teaching is 1 Corinthians 13. We often isolate this chapter—for example, it is most often read publicly at weddings. And yet love is at the heart of the healing of divisions caused by one part of the body thinking that its gifts or purpose is superior to another part of the body. Love is at the center of any biblical spirituality. John Wesley did not speak about holiness or perfection without speaking also about love (Mark 12). Paul writes of love as the "more excellent way" (KJV, NRSV) or "an even better way" (1 Cor 12:31 CEB) and "the greatest" gift (1 Cor 13:13). He also writes:

> Love is patient, love is kind, it isn't jealous, it doesn't brag, it isn't arrogant, it isn't rude, it doesn't seek its own advantage, it isn't irritable, it doesn't keep a record of complaints, it isn't happy with injustice, but it is happy with the truth. Love puts up with all things, trusts in all things, hopes for all things, endures all things. Love never fails. (1 Cor 13:4-8 CEB)

In practice, love makes life in community possible. In practice, love overcomes all that tears us apart. And in practice, love is the path toward holiness. We began as a holiness movement. How do we discover this power?

The Essential Unifying Power

The essential unifying power, of which Yuval Levin writes, is simply the assembly of all of the activities that we do together—ecumenical agreements, educational processes and institutions, prophetic statements, communication plans, mission initiatives, discipleship resources, publications—and the relationships among those who do this work. These activities are in fact astonishing, and many gifted persons devote much of their lives to them. And yet, they are at risk in the fracturing of the republic (denomination). They assume that we are a denomination. We cannot assume continuity. Nothing in our culture (national, global, ecclesial) undergirds continuity. We are in a disruptive moment—this is true in the United States, in Europe, in the Philippines, and in Africa.

A part of the motivation for doing the work of maximizing promise while minimizing danger is the preservation (and, yes, reformation) of the "unifying power" of our institutions. While institutions are often criticized, many (including the most vulnerable) flourish because of the resources provided by institutions—for example, equitable compensation, the national plans, theological education in central conferences, ministerial education fund, and the list could go on.

Our "foremost challenge" is in naming the positive good at the heart of our Dream—we believe that followers of Jesus, in the Wesleyan tradition in general but in The United Methodist Church more particularly, can work together to make disciples for the transformation of the world. We do this in many different ways—this is diversity and choice. But we must do the work in a much clearer and collaborative way. And we must recognize that polarization and division—where we are, if we are honest, most at home, within our own tribe—are the greatest threats to our continued common life. How do we recover the apostolic teaching that transforms divisions and factions into a diversity of gifts, granted to us for the common good?

───────────── ✚ ─────────────

Exaggerating the Differences

From studying *The Anatomy of Peace*[4] in a community or in a reading group, it's obvious and good to acknowledge that we seek a heart of peace with each other. Less obvious and more convicting is that to go to war with each other, we must exaggerate the differences between us.

A heart at peace searches for what we share in common. And for me, in relation to the church, that is the gospel, which is a gift to us.

What we share in common is that we have received a gift. The differences lie in what we do after we receive the gift. And that distinction, it seems, is one that the Giver has the right to make.

───────────────────────

The temptation might be to dominate the cultural (ecclesial, denominational) conversation, as a kind of will-to-power. We are so evenly divided, however, that this is not politically pragmatic, even if it were a morally worthy strategy. And finally we aspire to something more, and this aspiration is our own cooperation with the prayer of Jesus that we might be one, so that the world might believe (John 17).

---+---

An Exercise

How then might we, as leaders, build thriving subcultures in our teams, boards, and cabinets, in our spheres of influence and leadership, in delegations from the annual conferences, and together, toward a future that is less fractured and more united, and in alignment with God's dream for the people called Methodist? How can the local honor the global and vice versa?

JUST RESOLUTION AS AN EXPRESSION OF RESTORATIVE JUSTICE

Matthew 15

Who Has Been Harmed?

When a violation of the _Book of Discipline_ occurs, related to overlapping marks of LGBTQ and Christian (United Methodist) community and identity, we might begin with a question: Who has been harmed?

Possible answers include the following:

- Some persons define the harm in a direct way—a parishioner belongs to a church and senses that her liturgical space has been used for a political (or unbiblical) purpose.

- Some persons define the harm in a more indirect way—a United Methodist in one place describes confusion about interpretation of scripture or conceptions of holiness.

- And some persons focus instead on addressing the root causes of the harm; for example, a paragraph in the *Book of Discipline* that singles out a particular and isolated practice as incompatible with Christian teaching (BOD ¶161.f).

When harm has occurred, there is often a tendency to assign blame and seek justice. This justice focuses first on the person who has caused the offense, and for some, justice requires punishment, which is seen as the consequence of the behavior. In essence, accountability implies punishment. Thus a "just resolution" can look like a sequence of events: The victim has been harmed by the offender and has experienced pain; the resolution must include a corresponding experience of pain by the offender. In this way, we objectify the other; we do not see each other as persons, and this arises from a "heart at war" (see *The Anatomy of Peace* discussed in chapter eight).

A Heart at Peace

The alternative to a heart at war is a "heart at peace." In his commentary on Matthew's Gospel, Stanley Hauerwas reflects on the nature of Mary's pregnancy, which was a violation of the law, and Joseph's response:

> Unwilling to cause Mary distress, to expose her to public disgrace, he planned to dismiss her discreetly. Joseph, therefore, refused to act according to the law, but rather chose to act in a manner that Jesus himself would later exemplify in his attitude toward known sinners (Matt 9:10-13).[1]

In the institutional church, some are quite willing to see the other vilified publicly. And yet, when the person is someone we love, or when we are living in grace, can we not seek justice or judgment privately? If you were the offender, how would you hope to be treated? At our worst, we want justice for the stranger and grace for ourselves, our families, and our friends. At our best, we take no delight in the public disgrace of those who transgress the law.

At our worst, we live and lead from a heart at war. At our best, we live and lead from a heart at peace. Matthew 15 describes a conversation between Jesus and the religious leaders of his time about the traditions of the elders, in particular about the violation of laws (commandments). His response is to quote the prophet Isaiah ("This people honors me with their lips, but their hearts are far from me" [Matt 15:8 NRSV]). He then offers the insight that we are defiled by the words that we speak, which reveal the state of our hearts (15:18-19).

We begin from within, and we express the condition of our heart in speech. This speech matters; as Abraham Heschel notes, "words create worlds." Our world includes the systems where we live and lead. And these systems, in turn, come to shape and define us over time.

Our Western legal systems are often grounded in a heart at war, more rooted in criminal and retributive justice than restorative justice, in the laws that have been broken rather than the harm that has been done. The United Methodist Church has based its conception of justice and just resolutions on this model, with our complex system of a judicial council, trials, presiding officers in these trials (bishops) and conference chancellors (attorneys). Further, it is a model fashioned after the US justice system, even as the church itself has become more global (Africa, Philippines, Europe).

These legal and criminal justice systems are increasingly perceived as untenable and unsustainable in the United States. Consider the reality of mass incarceration, the inequity of legal representation, the prisons owned by corporations that charge the poor for food and supplies. Retributive justice has not been helpful in securing justice in The UMC. Trials are "to be regarded as an expedient of last resort" (BOD ¶2707), but they are the preferred method of behavior among those who have mastered this craft (often clergy with professional training or degrees in the law) and are most comfortable in this environment. And there is the occasional absurdity of those who publicly proclaim "no more trials" while privately insisting on a trial—which is a right within the present *Book of Discipline*.

✚

Courts

While we welcome and appreciate friends who are attorneys and judges in our congregations, the language of courts, judicial processes, and trials have no place in the church. These proceedings belong in the civil sphere. Where we need accountability, justice, and truth-telling, the scriptures ask us to go about this in a different way. I would remove every reference to judicial behavior and trials in the United Methodist *Book of Discipline*, and move accountability to the Board of Ordained Ministry (clergy), the Council of Bishops (bishops), or to the local church (laity).

Proposing and implementing an alternative Christian process for accountability opens the door to a wide range of responses. I am simply making a clear statement related to our polity, which I believe is not helping us with our internal relationships and our external mission. What we have, at present, is the reality of being conformed to the world. What we yearn for is a way of life transformed by the renewing of our minds (Rom 12).

The Present State of The United Methodist Church

In the present moment, the church includes within its membership (clergy and laity) persons who sharply disagree about understandings of human sexuality (orientation and practice) and ways to live together amidst the dissonance. The polity of the whole church is revised (or not) once every four years, often in a plenary session that occurs within a one-hour time period. Protest movements surround this conference and at times disrupt the deliberations. Regional bodies (annual conferences, boards of ordained ministry, and colleges of bishops) make statements that reflect the values of smaller and usually more homogeneous groups of people; this work is done with more ease, agreement, and clarity.

The Council of Bishops (COB) is often criticized for its lack of leadership in this conversation, even as the General Conference disperses authority to other bodies (clergy sessions, boards of ministry) or rejects the idea that a bishop could work exclusively ("set-apart") in this area. In addition, the COB is simply more global and complex in its nature than the regional bodies or advocacy groups. Lastly, our denominational media often become most stimulated by a courtroom, criminal, and legal-justice frame in its reporting on human sexuality; a quick internet search will bear this out.

This intricate web of persons, systems, and roles is not in itself the problem. I simply wonder if we do our work with a set of assumptions that may be neither helpful nor truthful. In *The Anatomy of Peace*, this is described as **collusion**.[2] We have become very sophisticated at sustaining conflict and creating systems that perpetuate conflict.

From Collusion to Covenant

In our unhealthy patterns of behavior, we are joined together via collusion: we bring out the worst in each other, we do harm to each other, and this mutual harm creates a bond between us. When we acknowledge this reality, and we do so in the words of our prayer of confession—"we have failed to be an obedient church"—and when we declare our intention to change (repentance), we are on a journey from collusion to covenant with each other. In United Methodism, these covenants are formed in public ways through baptism, membership, licensing, ordination, and consecration. These covenants are also renewed when we recite the words at Holy Communion, in our appeal to God to "Make us one with Christ, one with each other, and one in ministry to the world."

Unity, which is a gift from God, is also the fruit of the difficult work of moving beyond our tribalisms (our preferences, etc.) toward a relationship with and identity in the One who transcends every particularity. Such a covenant is built on trust—faith in God's faithfulness (Rom 3–4), and sharing of life (*koinonia*) with each other (Phil 1). This trust also includes our capacity to be trustworthy in regard to transparency, competence, and integrity.

Our affirmations of faith (creeds) are statements of trust. In this way, Wesleyan Christians are both conciliar and confessional; we are never one without the other—and so there is no truth without unity, or grace without truth, or unity without grace. In John 1:14-18, Jesus is described as the "tent of meeting," the glory of God among us, in the flesh. God is glorified whenever the followers of Jesus gather in his name and spirit and find themselves repeating his actions. The word *grace* rarely appears in John, but it reminds us of the gift of the light that is coming into the world, that shines in the darkness. Truth is not our usual sense of a belief to be affirmed or a standard to be upheld; instead, truth is a real, authentic experience.[3]

And lastly, grace is not contrasted to truth in these verses; grace and truth (embodied in the flesh, in Jesus, wherever we encounter him) are contrasted with the law. Moses had asked to see God; he was given the Torah, which is the way to life. And yet in Jesus, we see God, and in his life, which unfolds in John's Gospel, we see again and again the fullness of grace and truth.

Grace, Truth, and Unity

What if the grace/truth binary construction is inadequate, simply a religious way of having the more secular political conversation about compassion/responsibility? What if the more interesting conversation holds three concepts in tension: grace/truth/unity? How did we think we could have the John 1 conversation (grace/truth) without John 17 (unity)?

Jesus comes to embody the new covenant, full of grace and truth in contrast to and in fulfillment of the old covenant. The language of covenant is most fundamentally the acknowledgement that we live within a scarred history and amidst a broken world, and that we are in need of covenantal relationships. God has shown us the way, remaining faithful when we are faithless, providing strength in our weakness, seeking us when we would prefer not to be found, and never giving up on us. This is the lesson of the succession of prophets who come in the history of Israel, reminders of God's loyal, covenant faithfulness, refusing to end the divine-human relationship, and even, in the fullness of time, at the cost of the atoning (reconciling) sacrifice, who is the Lamb of God who takes away the sin of the world (John 1:29). The fullness of this covenant is both external and internal—the word that comes from beyond us, the law that is written on the heart (Jer 31–33) and the Spirit that gives life. And biblical covenant is always a paradox—constricting and life-giving, dying to self and rising to human flourishing, losing our lives and finding them.

Just Resolution: An Alternative Path

God is always seeking a way forward in the scriptures, a way beyond our brokenness and rebellion and estrangement. So how might this shape our covenant-making, covenant-breaking, and covenant renewal with each other? What if there is another way forward in seeking just resolutions? And what if this way is more rooted in restorative justice? We might begin not with a focus on violation of the *Book of Discipline* but on the harm that is caused in our connection (see *The Little Book of Restorative Justice*).[4] This leads us back to our first General Rule, to "do no harm." Here the church (usually a bishop or district superintendent) will begin by seeking to reframe the event—from a formal complaint regarding violation of the *Book of Discipline* to the implications for the connection, most often life in an annual conference or perhaps in a local church.

The bishop (or designated person) might begin with a fundamental question: How does the victim articulate the harm done? Both offender and victim (respondent and complainant) are involved in the process.

- Can the offending person acknowledge the harm done?

- Can the offending person adequately articulate, where appropriate, the root causes of the behavior to the person who has been harmed?

- Can the victim understand the root causes that motivate the offender?

- Can this be done, in The United Methodist Church, with a deep reading of scripture and tradition?

- Can we assume or articulate a common faith?

- Can we draw upon the rich values of the experience of God's grace and the journey toward holiness?

It may be assumed that the work of restorative justice is some form of avoidance. In reality, the work may become more difficult. In comparison, adversarial processes of law separate us and do not have restoration as a goal. If the divisions are too pronounced, we go our separate ways. Note this insight from two theologians in the Anglican communion, written in 2007 during the schism of the Episcopal Church in America:

> It has become painfully clear that those on both the left and the right have chosen to "walk apart." The prophets on the left claim the backing of divine providence that has placed them ahead of the pack. They are content to go it alone and simply wait for others to catch up. The prophets on the right claim to be the champions of orthodoxy—charged with maintaining a faithful church in the midst of "apostasy." They are content to go it alone and await the vindication of God. . . . The burden . . . is the obedient way—one that serves as a caution to the prophets on both the left and the right and a beacon to those for whom maintenance of communion constitutes a fundamental obligation.[5]

But the alternative path, a set of crucial conversations, even an "obedient way," might deepen our love for God and neighbor, which John Wesley defined as the process of sanctification.

New Ways to Seek Justice

This journey inspires a set of necessary questions at the outset:

- Are we willing to stay together in doing the work of restorative justice?

- In Parker Palmer's language, can we stay at the table with those whom we sense have betrayed us, as Jesus did with Judas?

- Can we walk with the offender in accepting the obligations inherent in his or her behavior?

- Can we begin not with the question, "How does the

other person need to change?" but with "How do I need to change?"

- Do all of the stakeholders see these actions as ways of addressing the harm and not as punishment?

- Can we articulate future expected behaviors?

- Can we reintegrate offenders and victims back into the community (conference, connection)?

- Throughout, can we show respect to everyone involved?

- Can a model of restorative justice serve and contribute to the healing of the church?

John 13 and Betrayal

We are created for community, and we have a fundamental need and desire for relationships. And yet, if we live long enough we will inevitably be harmed by other people, or the people we love will be damaged. If we are honest, through the evil we have done, or the good we have left undone, we will also damage and harm other people.

These two realities exist in tension with each other: our need for community, and the behaviors that lead us away from relationships with each other. The Quaker contemplative and social activist Parker Palmer offers a compelling insight. It is one prompted by the question of how Jesus could stay at the table with Judas and the other disciples in the awareness of their betrayal of him:

> Community is not so much a demonstration of heaven as it is a via negativa to God. We will always be disillusioned by community. But in the spiritual life disillusionment is a good thing: it means losing our illusions about ourselves and each other. As

those illusions fall away we will be able to see reality and truth more clearly. And the truth is that we can rely on God to make community among us even—and especially—when our own efforts fail.... And here is the paradox: as we become disillusioned with community and more dependent on God, we become more available for true community with each other.... Seeing ourselves and each other clearly, yet seeing God's continual healing presence among us, we can begin to experience the fruits of the Spirit with each other: love, joy, peace, patience, kindness, goodness and gentleness.[6]

Accountability or Punishment?

Jesus's command of the disciples (and us!) to love each other is given not in an environment of naiveté and innocence. His is a radical call to integrate our human nature—in this instance, betrayal—and our human destiny: to build the beloved community of sinners, present at the table only through the grace of the One who created us, who knows us completely, and yet who loves us, and believes, against all odds, that we might love each other.

In our pursuit of mercy and justice, compassion and righteousness, may we stay at the table with each other. May those who welcome LGBTQ persons, march for the unborn, campaign for the trafficked, keep vigil for the condemned, stand with the farmworkers, and provide sanctuary for the abused feast together in the presence of the Lord. And may we know it to be a table of sacrifice and love: Jesus, crucified and risen, is with us on this evening.

What might a just resolution look like based on these practices? There might be real accountability rather than punishment. There might be a greater acknowledgement of both the effect of actions outside of the BOD on Christians who interpret scripture and human sexuality within the traditional consensus of the ecumenical church, and the effect of our present BOD language in the lives of individuals, families, and allies in the LGBTQ community. Each sees itself, at present, as a (or the) victim.

The present legal and criminal justice system, as it has been incorporated, used, and misused by The United Methodist Church, is designed precisely for the results we are currently experiencing: "when our hearts go to war, we have chosen it."[7] If the way forward includes a connection of United Methodists, I am persuaded that we will need to discover: (1) new ways of seeking justice, and (2) new ways of being with each other. I am also aware that we will need to reconcile our divergent understandings of holiness.

Why We Disagree

A part of our challenge is that, in addition to our divergent understandings of holiness, we may have two distinct conceptions of church. These conceptions of church have been present in American Methodism for at least two hundred years, and the seeds may be seen in the earliest practice of British Methodism.

One understanding is a *separatist* church, which views holiness as a calling that separates us from the world—"come out from among them and be separated" (2 Cor 6:17 CEB). Here holiness is a quality that distinguishes us from the world.

A second understanding is an *activist* church, which understands holiness as a movement for change in an unjust world. The boundaries between church and society are blurred, with the "wheat and weeds" growing together (Matt 13) until God's final judgment.

At times, a denomination is able to hold these two conceptions of church in tension. And at times, and in recent experience of American mainline Christianity, there is fragmentation
and division.

The division may finally be the result of clearly articulated
values that are not compatible. And the division may also be the
result of how leaders of the two conceptions of church do harm
to each other. My delineation of the two conceptions above are a
great simplification, and yet in every congregation I served across
twenty-eight years there were persons who embodied them.

And so, with the recent consecration of a practicing lesbian
bishop, there are sharply different interpretations. One part of
the church sees this as a significant step toward separation, and
the recent Episcopal/Anglican experience or the Presbyterian
(PCUSA) experience provides a blueprint. Another part of the
church views this as a historical breakthrough, a matter of justice
and inclusion.

The resulting question is whether these two conceptions of
church can co-exist. This, it seems to me, remains the work of the
Commission on the Way Forward that arose through the General Conference in 2016. We are asking for time and patience
to do this work faithfully and in a way that does as little harm
as possible to our connection. We see these movements coming
into sharper definition, and yet we hear from significant voices in
the church that do not wish to be defined by either but wish to
remain in connection with each other and seek a way forward in
our mission with LGBTQ human beings faithfully serving in our
midst.

An Interim Witness: To Do No Harm, To Attain a Heart at Peace

Some time ago I came across this phrase in the *Rule of Taizé*:

Never resign yourself to the scandal of the separation of Christians who so readily profess love for their neighbor and yet remain divided. Make the unity of the body of Christ your passionate concern.

As a Wesleyan Christian, I have come to see over time that our journey to holiness necessarily involves the love of God and neighbor. Love of neighbor for John Wesley was an essential facet of the definition of sanctification (see his sermon "The Almost Christian"). Our divergent understandings of holiness—as either the reign of God, of which greater inclusiveness is a sign, or a set-apart righteousness, of which sexual purity is yet a different sign—must submit themselves a call to unity, even in an interim time. Indeed, from the perspective of the biblical witness, we are always living "between the times."

But in the interim, must we really walk apart? Is such an outcome a given, in a single attempt at a just resolution or in the larger conversation about our denominational future? Can we profess love for our neighbor and remain divided? Can we seek to attain a heart at peace and resist the temptation to a heart at war, which is, in Hebrew idiom, "hardness of heart" (that is, stubbornness)? Can we imagine a new way "to do justice, embrace faithful love, and walk humbly with God" (Mic 6:8 CEB), attentive to connection between the first question of restorative justice—"who has been harmed?" and our first General Rule—"to do no harm"?

109

In the present moment, the way we do the work of justice and just resolution, far from being a distraction, is a sign of our witness to each other and to those beyond us, that we are indeed becoming disciples of Jesus Christ for the transformation of the world.

------------------------------ ✚ ------------------------------

An Exercise

With whom do you find it most difficult to stay in relationship?

Who are the persons excluded from our tables and why?

Can you reflect on an experience of deep disillusionment? And can you have a conversation with Jesus about it?

Prayer

In the breaking of bread, in the pouring of the cup,
    and in the offering of our lives on behalf of others,
    may we live in communion with you,
    loving Jesus, and each other. Amen.

Chapter Ten

BRIDGES

John 17

Florida, where I live, is a beautiful state, a long peninsula situated between the Atlantic Ocean and the Gulf of Mexico. It is also covered with bodies of water, lakes, rivers, and intercoastal waterways. We were attracted to this place because of water and nearness to it. We have called this a fountain of life.

The tradition of American evangelicalism is closely aligned with camp meetings and arbors that were located near sources of water, perhaps for baptism. And, farther back, the holiest sites of our own tradition are near sources of water—Jacob's Well, the Galilee Sea, the Jordan River, the Siloam Pool. Waters were also places of ritual cleansing and healing, as with the *mikveh* baths of early Judaism.

Bridges

Florida is a state connected by bridges. Some of them are iconic, like the Seven Mile Bridge in the Keys. Others are lesser known. I have traveled back and forth across Florida and have met amazing people, people who follow Jesus, people who love their churches, people who are transformational leaders in their communities. This for me is the itineracy. Not staying in one place but crossing these bridges are necessary journeys if I am to really be in the presence of the people of the annual conference.

As the bishop of Florida, I serve a very diverse state: Orlando and Miami are among the most progressive cities on the planet; Jacksonville and Sarasota are very traditional; Tallahassee and Gainesville are university towns. These cities are connected across this lovely state by a series of bridges.

As a moderator of the Commission on a Way Forward, I served with the thirty-two members who met together over a two-year period. They did sacrificial, extraordinary work on behalf of the denomination. They crossed bridges of language, culture, sexual orientation, theology, geography, and age. They did this because they are women and men of deep faith and profound love for their church. Many of us traveled across bridges that others have imagined and constructed. And yet many will also need to repair some of these bridges and build new ones. Rowan Williams reflects on bridges as an image for the priesthood in this way:

> A priest is somebody who interprets God and humanity to each other. A priest is somebody who builds bridges between God and humanity when that relationship has been wrecked: somebody who by offering sacrifice to God re-creates a shattered relationship. Of Jesus's priestly role I need hardly speak of that connection. As baptized people are drawn into the priestliness of Jesus, they are called upon to mend shattered relationships between God and the world, through the power of Christ and his Spirit. As baptized people, we are in the business of building bridges. We are in the business, once again, of seeing situations where there is breakage, damage and disorder, and bringing into these situations the power of God in Jesus Christ and the Holy Spirit in order to rebuild something.[1]

Williams is reflecting on John 17, which can be called the priestly prayer of Jesus.

> When Jesus finished saying these things, he looked up to heaven and said, "Father, the time has come. Glorify your Son, so that the Son can glorify you. You gave him authority over everyone so that he could give eternal life to everyone you gave him. This is eternal life: to know you, the only true God, and Jesus Christ whom you sent. I have glorified you on earth by finishing the work you gave me to do. Now, Father, glorify me in your presence with the glory I shared with you before the world was created." (John 17:1-5 CEB)

> I pray they will be one, Father, just as you are in me and I am in you. I pray that they also will be in us, so that the world will believe that you sent me. I've given them the glory that you gave me so that they can be one just as we are one. I'm in them and you are in me so that they will be made perfectly one. Then the world will know that you sent me and that you have loved them just as you loved me. (John 17:21-23 CEB)

The gospel teaches us, through words and actions, that Jesus himself is the bridge between God and humanity. He unites the schism caused by our sin. He races toward us when we had left home. He forgives us when we have betrayed him. He dies for us in our state of sinfulness. He reconciles the world to himself. As he is lifted up, he draws all people to himself.

All who take the name of Jesus in baptism are called to become bridges who connect God and the people he has created in his image, the world that he loves, the creation that he speaks into being. In baptism, all of us are immersed into the priestly ministry of Jesus.

Behind the general ministry of all Christians, the role of the representative minister—the elder, the deacon, the local pastor—is twofold:

- first, to remind the people we serve that they are a priesthood of believers;

- second, to embody the repairing and building of bridges in our own ministries.

Intercession

In John 17, Jesus speaks to the church through the form of prayer, more precisely, through intercession. In one moving passage of Dietrich Bonhoeffer's *Life Together*, the theologian and martyr says,

> A pastor should never complain about her congregation, certainly never to other people, but also not to God. A congregation has not been entrusted to her in order that she should become its accuser before God and men.... Let the pastor rather accuse himself for his unbelief. Let him pray to God for an understanding of his own failure and his particular sin, and pray that he may not wrong his brothers and sisters. Let us, in the consciousness of our own guilt, make intercession for our brothers and sisters. Let us do what we are committed to do, and thank God.

———————— ✚ ————————

Imagine, for a moment, that we substituted the word *denomination* for the word *congregation* in Bonhoeffer's reflection!

We have been called to repair and build bridges for such a time as this. It would be easier not to build a bridge. It would be easier to stay on our side of whatever our preference or position or perspective might be.

But we have been set apart as lay leaders or clergy for a different purpose. We are set apart to do this very work. John 17 is an extended teaching of Jesus, and in the words of the missionary theologian Lesslie Newbigin, it accomplishes two objectives:

- He reminds the disciples that they are participating in the fulfillment of the great promise, that the dwelling of God will be with his people.
- He sends the disciples into the world to continue the mission for which Jesus came from the Father.[2]

The Meaning of Consecration

After praying, Jesus consecrates the disciples. To be consecrated means to be set apart. Many years ago, a mentor was talking to me about the role of bishop. He said, "It is a consecration, not a coronation." It is less about hierarchy and more about being set apart. We have been called by the church to invest the most precious resource we have—our lives—in this work. That is consecration. And why are we consecrated? To be an outward and visible sign, so that the world will believe.

Jesus prays for us, dies for us, rises for us, and lives in us so that the world will believe. We dedicate bridges. We consecrate lives. From a human point of view, we complain. In the spirit, we intercede. And in our intercession, we join in a prayer that has already begun, a prayer for us and for "all sorts and conditions of men and women," to paraphrase the *Book of Common Prayer*.

---------------- ✚ ----------------

If we see Him alone, we do not see Him at all. If we see Him, we see with and around Him in ever-widening circles, His disciples, the people, His enemies, and the countless millions who have not yet heard His name. We see Him as theirs, determined by them and for them, belonging to each and every one of them.[3]

Our Shared Convictions and Why They Matter

In Donald Miller's *Building a StoryBrand*,[4] he insists that every great story has a main character. In the story I have told, the main character is not The United Methodist Church, the Council of Bishops, or the Commission on a Way Forward. The main character is not our favorite renewal or advocacy group.

Who then would be the main character in this narrative?

My short list of answers to this question would include the following:

- the evangelical pastor who has sacrificed to build a strong church

- the lesbian who has been a part of the UMC her whole life

- the young adult clergy who wonders if there will be a church to serve in

- the African Christian who wants to continue to do life-saving work

In your own imagination, can you describe a main character? These main characters have something in common: they all live with some kind of fear. It is not that one kind of person has a fear. In each story there is a fear.

- The pastor wonders if all of the life's work will be diminished because of conflict.

- The LGBTQ person wonders if this was ever really her church.

- The young adult clergy wonders if there will be a way to express ministry.

- The African leader wonders if the resources will be there to continue.

There are multiple main characters in the story of The United Methodist Church. Much social media would lead us to believe that there is only one main character, one grievance to be addressed, one conclusion to be reached. And yet, what if it is more complex than this?

An Exercise

I encourage you to take the time, only a few minutes, to view the compelling Ted Talk, "The Danger of a Single Story" by Nigerian storyteller Chimamanda Adichie. Over fifteen million people have watched this video. She writes, "When we reject the single story, when we realize that there is never a single story about any place, we regain a kind of paradise!"[5] How does such wisdom speak to a global church that is seeking a way forward?

We are a profoundly diverse global church with fifteen million members on four continents. What could possibly unite us? And how can we write a *Book of Discipline* for multiple stories? We have many compelling stories. There are many significant voices, even main characters in our denomination. And, at the same time, there are shared convictions. And these shared convictions can sustain us in finding a way forward together.

Generous Orthodoxy Connects All People with the Saving Grace of Jesus Christ

I want to be faithful to the scriptures and the Christian tradition, as I understand them. I want to submit to the witness of the gospel within the scriptures, and the stream of tradition as it has flowed through the centuries. This understanding shapes many of the spiritual practices that are at the heart of my discipleship:

- I want to learn the scriptures and read them each day.

- I say the Apostles' and Nicene Creeds.

- My beliefs are guided by the Articles of Religion and the Confession of Faith.

- My behaviors are governed by the General Rules.

- I have received the prevenient, justifying, and sanctifying grace of God.

- I love to sing the Wesley hymns (such as "And Can It Be," "A Charge to Keep," "O For a Thousand Tongues to Sing," and "Love Divine, All Loves Excelling").

118

- I have been accountable to and supported in small groups of a few trusted friends (class and band meetings).

- I participate in services of baptism and Eucharist.

- I am engaged in works of piety, mercy, and justice.

- I share in a common ministry exercised by clergy and laity, and my church recognizes the orders of clergy in the pan-Methodist family (AME, AME Zion, CME).

- I know and remember our shared Methodist/Wesleyan history, even with our divisions and, yes, our failures.

- I have been engaged in shared mission work and know that God sends us from everywhere to everywhere.

- I embrace a connectional way of life and leadership that includes forms of (1) superintendency for the purpose of accountability to the mission, (2) itineracy for the purpose of multiplication of mission, and (3) conferencing for the purpose of inspiration, support and governance.

- I assume that theology has practical (moral) implications, that is, "practical divinity" or "lived theology" or "faith working through love."

- I desire to share this faith in healthy and positive ways; as Wesleyans, we speak more of the love than the wrath of God.

I also want to love the people who God has placed in my path. We cannot love God, whom we have never seen, if we do not love our brother or sister, whom we have seen (1 John 4). I want the church to be open to all people, the grace of God for all people, the ministry of the church for all people. I have been blessed by the courage and gifts of LGBTQ members of every church, and I have known more closely LGBTQ persons who are on the same journey of holiness that I am on.

I want to bridge these two realities—a generously orthodox faith and the people God has created and loves, and among them persons in the LGBTQ community. That there is now an impasse is the problem. The way forward, I am convinced, is found in the substance of our faith, our own scriptures and traditions, if we will hear them carefully and teach them faithfully. It is nothing more, nor less, than "offering them Christ!" And in the process of offering them Christ we will discover our own salvation!

I believe many people want to believe in God our Father, who is gracious and merciful, patient and full of faithful love. I believe that many want to follow Jesus Christ, who crossed all kinds of boundaries as the embodiment of this grace and who seemed to interpret the Torah in life-giving and gracious ways. And I believe many experience the indwelling Holy Spirit, who encourages and convicts and guides us into the truth.

Summary

- A generously orthodox faith and trust in God, through Jesus Christ, in the Holy Spirit, is the bridge that can connect us. It is not a wall that divides us.

- A generously orthodox faith can create the generative space where covenant keepers, justice-seekers and those passionate about unity can walk together (chapter one).

- A generously orthodox faith is rooted in the radical grace that saves us and that same radical grace that breaks down the walls of hostility between us (chapter two).

- A generously orthodox faith is rooted in our best loved stories, such as Jesus's parable of the free and infinite grace of the parent who welcomes the child home (chapter three).

- A generously orthodox faith can help us to discern the movement of the Holy Spirit (chapter four).

- A generously orthodox faith is rooted in a Wesleyan understanding of the grace of God (chapter five).

- A generously orthodox faith teaches us to be patient with one another (chapter six).

- A generously orthodox faith sustains us in the demanding but essential work of reconciliation (chapter seven).

- A generously orthodox faith reminds us that the apostles taught the early church to see our differences as gifts (chapter eight).

- A generously orthodox faith is a resource to resolve complaints and conflict in restorative and non-punitive ways (chapter nine).

- A generously orthodox faith is the church's bridge toward both unity and community with all persons, including those with LGBTQ identity (chapter ten).

As a relatively new Christian in my late teens, I was taught to share "the bridge," which was a visual image of the way of salvation. On one side was God, in his holiness. On the other side was humanity, in our sinfulness. The separation, the chasm, could only be bridged by Jesus Christ, who was both God and a human being.

I was taught to share this visual image with persons I had never met. Some were interested. Others less so. In a simple way, it framed a way of connecting us with the agenda of God, which was and is to offer us salvation and new life.

The image of the bridge stays with me. I continue to claim it. And yet I live in an admittedly more complex world. God is inviting us to cross a bridge, to take one step and then another, often beyond our comfort zones, as people who have received the gift of faith in Jesus Christ, and yet who know, deep within, that the gift is not for ourselves.

The way forward is not only about the institution of the church. Institutions are important. They help us to share in mission. They secure the rights of the less privileged. When we lose an institution, we know suddenly that we had taken much of its value for granted.

And yet the way forward has always been the Way of the Lord, the road traveled by God's pilgrim people, who hear the clear and compelling voice of Jesus, saying "Follow me." The way forward is about the wideness of God's mercy, which, as the hymn continues, is broader than the measure of our minds.

O God,
Your intention to give exceeds our readiness to receive.
Your boundless love is restricted by our small vessels.
Your generosity far exceeds our responding reception.
Your richness is restrained by our poverty of expectation.
Your expansiveness is channeled through our small hearts.
Enlarge our capacity.
Increase our receptivity.
Open us to your full life.
Make us more able to receive your generous grace.
Amen.[6]

TO EMBRACE THE WIDENESS OF GOD'S MERCY IS TO BE ONE, HOLY, CATHOLIC, AND APOSTOLIC

The living church is a priesthood of believers. Our faithful witness and presence helps to mend shattered lives and relationships. Our strength and confidence is rooted in the marks of the church, proclaimed in the Nicene Creed. A generously orthodox church is *one, holy, catholic,* and *apostolic.* Such a church will necessarily draw deeply from scripture and tradition. In this way we are one and holy. And such a church will offer the gospel (good news) to all people in the coming generations, and in this manner we will be catholic and apostolic.

The church that offers the gift of abundant grace to all is not a departure from God's intention. Such a church approximates the radical, indiscriminate, and expansive mission that we read about in the gospels and that was proclaimed in the apostolic witness.

The marks of the church call us to embrace the wideness of God's mercy. At our best, these have been and are the shared convictions of United Methodists.

+The church is one.

The unity of the church is grounded in the One God (Deut 6), affirmed by Jesus (Mark 12), and in the teachings of the apostles in Ephesians 4 (one Lord, one faith, one baptism). This unity is a gift of God (1 Cor 12), and is never a human achievement, right, or claim. The practical expression of unity is the love of God and neighbor (which is also the practical expression of holiness). Our complacency with division indicates a lack of love and is finally a barrier to the mission of the gospel in the midst of unbelief; I pray we hear Jesus saying in John 17, that they may be one, so that the world will believe that you have sent me. Thus unity needs to be visible.

It is true we are connected with each other in the one body. When one suffers, all suffer. When one rejoices, all rejoice. In The United Methodist Church we have a term for this: the *connection*. It expresses our unity, our oneness. In The UMC, we might identify the instruments of our unity as the itineracy of preachers, the superintendency, which includes bishops and Christian conferencing.

We are one. But it goes far beyond being a Methodist. The one body of Christ includes all who profess the name of Jesus: Catholic to Pentecostal, house church to cathedral, urban to rural, conservative and liberal, if we must use those words! There are not many churches; there is one church, because there is one Lord, one faith, one baptism.

+The church is holy.

Is the church holy? I remember early in our ministry an evening in which my wife Pam and I had dinner with two women (sisters) who were the daughters of a minister and had grown up in a parsonage. It was an evening I will never forget. They recalled, through our four-hour conversation, one negative experience after another across a number of churches—judgmentalism, mistreatment, and inhumanity. I left wondering, *What am I getting myself into?*

Of course, the church is a human institution, and most of us are some combination of saint and sinner. The church's sins are often spread out before the public: clergy misconduct, financial scandal, racism, exclusion, unbelief. Some of our sins are more hidden: competition with other churches or consumerism with religious experience, which is the dark side of the attractional church, a dominant way of functioning in a market economy.

So what does it mean to say that the church is holy? The church as an ideal is holy, and yet even scripture confesses that "we have this treasure [of the gospel] in clay pots" (2 Cor 4:7 CEB). One dimension of this holiness is that the church is set apart for a particular purpose; this is variously defined as word and sacrament, the body of Christ, and as a sign and foretaste of the kingdom of God. This holiness is both personal and social, evidenced by prayer and service, action and contemplation.

The pursuit of holiness requires an inner strength, a discipline. But this is a mark of the authentic church; Paul came back to this, over and over again, in 1 Corinthians. In an immoral culture, he called the followers of Jesus to holiness, and in a deeply divided society he reminded those who had been baptized that they were one.

+The church is catholic.

I remember attending church as a teenager, and we would come to the place in the Apostles' Creed where we would say "I believe in the Holy Catholic Church," and there was always a slight hesitancy in that Deep South congregation. In our hymnal there was an asterisk beside the word *catholic*, with the explanation at the bottom of the page that it meant "universal." And while we may not always understand what we mean by "catholic church" when we say those words, they are deeply embedded in our tradition as Methodists.

As mentioned earlier, one of John Wesley's most famous sermons is "The Catholic Spirit." The church is catholic, or universal, in that its core identity is found in the whole and not merely in the fragments of its local expression. This resonates with Paul's image of the body in 1 Corinthians 12 and his meditation on love in 1 Corinthians 13. To do the work of God is, in the language of the preamble to *A Gift to The World* (the United Methodist proposal for full communion with The Episcopal Church), "to bring our churches into closer partnership [*koinonia*] in the mission and witness to the love of God."

+The church is apostolic.

The church is apostolic as its life is traced to the teachings of the apostles. This differs from literal apostolic succession, with the Pope being the historical successor of Peter in the New Testament. Although this would be the conviction of Catholics, we honor this tradition about apostolic teaching. The church is a family tree whose roots go down deeply into the apostles teaching about the life, the death, and the resurrection of Jesus, and how this event has already changed the world. In Acts 2:42, the early "believers devoted themselves to the apostles' teaching, to the community, to their shared meals, and to their prayers."

What was the apostles' teaching? Well, they did have a need to answer that question, and so these short summaries circulated, from generation to generation, first in creeds within the New Testament itself, later in the Nicene Creed, and then the Apostles' Creed. The tradition of the apostles certainly has, as its core, the Orthodox, Catholic, and Anglican expressions, and each stream has shaped the Wesleyan movement. This living tradition contains many of the resources that sustain our faith; at the same time, there is always a need for reformation, for prophetic witness, for what Greg Jones calls "traditioned innovation."[1]

And so we might then ask: What are the missional needs that call for our adaptation and reformation? We can look back and see Methodism adapting to new geographies and avoiding actions that would have required prophetic courage, as in our complicity in systemic racism.

What are the present cries for justice that require our adaptation? This is clearly at the heart of our conversations about human sexuality, our engagement with LGBTQ persons in our midst, and the question of their full inclusion.

The church is apostolic as it carries on the teaching of the apostles, but it has another meaning. To be an apostle is literally to be "sent" into the world. "As the Father sent me," Jesus says in John 20, "so I am sending you." The missiologist Dana Robert notes that there are more than two hundred references to the mission of being sent in the New Testament, rooted in the Greek verb *apostellein*.[2] The mission of The United Methodist Church is "to make disciples of Jesus Christ for the transformation of the world." We acknowledge in our thinking about mission that we are sent from "everywhere to everywhere." The global nature of our churches—in some sense the fruit of the apostolic mission—is also at the heart of many of our internal divisions, and especially around understandings of human sexuality.

In the fractured human community that is The United Methodist Church, one expression of our body is seeking to define itself (in an over-and-against way) as the church that is *one, holy, catholic,* and *apostolic.* And the inference is that another stream of this same church is not.

Our future vitality will be determined by how the pilgrimage to holiness remains our calling. This was our original purpose and remains our gift to the larger church. We will need to quickly confess that such a holiness is not arrogance or separation. Instead, holiness is the love of God—searching the scriptures, kneeling to receive the bread that is always our urgent need, singing the hymns of Charles Wesley, and loving our neighbor—which is increasingly the healing of divisions in a violent and fractured nation and a fragmented and divided church.

Our future unity will also be shaped in part by how we define holiness. I have been an eyewitness to the reality that persons of LGBTQ identity are on the same journey to holiness that I am on. They stand in need of the grace of God, as I do. They are present in our churches. Their testimonies are often strikingly similar to those of more traditional orientations. This is their faith and ours, their church and ours. It is a beautiful, generously orthodox faith, one that depends on the truth of the scripture to name our God as "merciful and compassionate, very patient, full of faithful love" (Ps 145:8; Joel 2:13 CEB).

NOTES

Preface

1. "Forming Scriptural Imagination": A Panel Discussion with Richard Hays, Ellen Davis, and Stanley Hauerwas at Duke Divinity School, February 11, 2013, https://www.youtube.com /watch?v=hTOVoWbRc0A.

1. Generous Orthodoxy

1. For the significance of "both/and," I am indebted to Paul Chilcote, *Recapturing the Wesleys' Vision* (Downers Grove, IL: IVP Academic, 2004).

2. Hans Frei, "Response to 'Narrative Theology: An Evangelical Appraisal,'" *Trinity Journal* (Spring 1987): 21. See also Brian McLaren, *A Generous Orthodoxy* (Grand Rapids: Zondervan, 2006).

3. Fleming Rutledge, "What Is Generous Orthodoxy? A Statement of Purpose," www.generousorthodoxy.org.

4. Malcolm Gladwell, "Generous Orthodoxy," August 10, 2016, *Revisionist History*, Panoply Media, podcast, 33:00, http:// revisionisthistory.com/episodes/09-generous-orthodoxy.

5. I am aware of public responses to my recent reflection on generous orthodoxy by David F. Watson ("The Innate Generosity of Orthodoxy, David F. Watson, August 15, 2017, https://david fwatson.me/2017/08/15/the-innate-generosity-of-orthodoxy/) and Joel Watts ("Generous Orthodoxy? A Reply to Bishop Carter," *Unsettled Christianity*, August 14, 2017, http://unsettledchristianity .com/generous-orthodoxy-reply-bishop-carter/). I share their

defense of a high Christology and appreciation of the great tradition; I respectfully differ in seeking to channel more of my energies in defining an orthodoxy that is generous in the pursuit of the unity of the church.

6. See The Arbinger Institute's *The Anatomy of Peace: Resolving the Heart of Conflict* (Oakland, CA: Berrett-Koehler, 2006). This has been a primary text of the Commission on a Way Forward of The United Methodist Church.

7. For the imagery of streams of theological tradition, see Thomas Langford, *Practical Divinity: Theology in the Wesleyan Tradition,* vol. 1 (Nashville: Abingdon, 1998).

8. Chilcote, *Recapturing the Wesleys' Vision,* 98.

9. The covenant, adopted by the thirty-two commissioners from four continents, is posted at www.umc.org/who-we-are /commission-on-a-way-forward-about-us.

10. Stanley Hauerwas, "Which Church? What Unity? Or, An Attempt to Say What I May Think about the Future of Christian Unity," in *Approaching the End: Eschatological Reflections on Church, Politics and Life* (Grand Rapids: Eerdmans, 2014), 109.

11. For a definition and picture of a Venn diagram, see https://en.wikipedia.org/wiki/Venn_diagram. Most often, a Venn diagram employs circles and the relationships of terms or groups of people in which some space overlaps and some does not.

12. I have benefitted from the reflection of Alan Hirsch and Michael Frost on "green spaces" that are both/and in character and combine story and context. See *The Shaping of Things To Come* (Peabody, MA: Hendrickson, 2003), 27–28.

13. This can be accessed at the site www.umc.org/who-we-are /commission-on-a-way-forward-about-us.

14. Chilcote, *Recapturing the Wesleys' Vision,* 16.

15. For this reason, the work of reconciliation—among races, across economic lines, amidst theological differences, with persons of LGBTQ identity—is not an interruption or obstacle to our mission; these may be critical teaching contexts that cry out

for the deep resources and convictions of biblical faith and Wesleyan tradition.

2. Confessing and Reconciling

1. Parker Palmer, *Healing the Heart of Democracy* (San Francisco: Jossey-Bass, 2011), 166.

2. Jack Jackson, "Breaking Up Is Hard, but Right Thing for the UMC," *The United Methodist Reporter*, October 19, 2012, http://unitedmethodistreporter.com/2012/10/19/breaking-up -is-hard-but-right-thing-for-the-umc/.

3. Wisdom from my longtime friend and spiritual director, Bob Tuttle.

4. "Leadership taking the shape of a cruciform life" is a phrase from the teaching of the theologian Robert Cushman.

3. So Free, So Infinite His Grace

1. John Wesley, "The Image of God," *The Sermons of John Wesley*, ed. Kenneth Collins and Jason Vickers (Nashville: Abingdon, 2013), 7.

2. Charles Wesley, "And Can It Be," *United Methodist Hymnal* (Nashville: The United Methodist Publishing House, 1989), no. 363.

3. Rembrandt, *The Return of the Prodigal Son*, 1661–1669, oil on canvas, 262 x 205 cm, Hermitage Museum, Saint Petersburg, https://en.wikipedia.org/wiki/Parable_of_the_Prodigal_Son #/media/File:Rembrandt_Harmensz_van_Rijn_-_Return_of _the_Prodigal_Son_-_Google_Art_Project.jpg. I recommend Henri Nouwen's *The Return of the Prodigal Son: A Story of Homecoming* (New York: Image/Doubleday, 1994).

4. Discerning the Movement of the Holy Spirit

1. "Renunciation of Sin and Profession of Faith," *The United Methodist Hymnal*, (Nashville: The United Methodist Publishing House, 1989), 34.

2. Luke the historian does not omit the real and human experience of gathered Gentile adults, recently converted to the Way of Jesus through the power of the Holy Spirit, who, when they hear the news that they will not have to undergo circumcision, "rejoiced at the exhortation" (15:31 NRSV)!

3. The Message paraphrases this as "to guard the morality of sex and marriage."

4. Luke Johnson, *Sacra Pagina: The Acts of the Apostles* (Collegeville, MN: Liturgical Press, 1992); see also Jaroslav Pelikan, *Brazos Theological Commentary on the Bible: Acts* (Grand Rapids: Brazos, 1995).

5. The linkage between the Greek word *porneia* and the pervasiveness of pornography cannot be lost on us, as well as pornography's destructive effect on lives and ministries among persons of all sexual orientations.

6. See Luke Johnson, *Scripture and Discernment: Decision Making in the Church* (Nashville: Abingdon, 1995), and Bill T. Arnold, "Acts 15 Doesn't Mean What You Think It Means," *Seedbed*, March 27, 2014, www.seedbed.com/acts-15-doesnt-mean-think-means/.

7. Johnson, *Scripture and Discernment*, 90.

5. God Hath Bid All Humankind

1. Lesslie Newbigin, *The Household of God* (London: SCM Press, 1953), 105.

2. Thomas Langford, *Doctrine and Theology in The United Methodist Church* (Nashville: Abingdon, 1991), 204.

3. Hamilton and Slaughter urged, "We believe that the question of homosexuality is virtually irresolvable at General Conference. Maintaining our current position will force progressives to continue to violate the *Discipline* as a matter of conscience. Reversing the position at General Conference would force hundreds of thousands of our conservative members to leave the denomination as a matter of conscience, with devastating consequences to many of our churches, and in turn, to our shared mission and ministry

together. We believe there is a better way forward than the current impasse or the division of The United Methodist Church." Proposed Amendment by Substitution for Calendar Item 513 (Daily Christian Advocate page number 2367), Petition Number 21032 (Advanced Daily Christian Advocate page number 270) of the 2012 General Conference of The United Methodist Church. For a later reflection by Adam Hamilton, see "On Homosexuality, Many Christians Get the Bible Wrong," *Washington Post*, February 13, 2013.

4. See John Wesley's "A Catholic Spirit" (1872) at http://wesley .nnu.edu/john-wesley/the-sermons-of-john-wesley-1872-edition /sermon-39-catholic-spirit/

5. Richard Hays, *The Moral Vision of the New Testament* (San Francisco: HarperSanFrancisco, 1996), 391.

6. A Catholic Spirit Reconsidered

1. Thomas Merton, *The Sign of Jonas* (New York: Harcourt Brace, 1953), 10.

2. Dietrich Bonhoeffer, *Life Together* (New York: Harper and Row, 1954), 26.

3. Reinhold Niebuhr, *Justice and Mercy* (New York: Harper and Row, 1974), 36.

4. *The Book of Discipline of The United Methodist Church* (Nashville: United Methodist Publishing House, 2016), paragraph 136. I am grateful to Sue Haupert-Johnson for guiding me to this passage.

5. For a contemporary reflection, see Steve Harper's study of "The Character of a Methodist" in *Five Marks of a Methodist* (Nashville: Abingdon, 2016).

6. *The Sermons of John Wesley*, 426.

7. The address is included in *Vision and Supervision: A Sourcebook of Significant Documents of the Council of Bishops of the United Methodist Church*, edited by James Mathews and William Odeon (Nashville: Abingdon, 2003), 160.

8. Note the excellent work more recently of Kendall Soulen, "Should United Methodists View Homosexual Conduct as a Matter of Status Confessionis?" in *Unity of the Church and Human Sexuality* (Nashville: GBHEM, 2018), 347ff. Soulen also reflects on the possibility of "conscientious disagreement in unity."

9. Lesslie Newbigin, *The Household of God* (London: SCM Press, 1953), 133.

7. We Do Not Lose Heart

1. Jelani Cobb, "Inside the Trial of Dylann Roof," *The New Yorker*, February 6, 2017, https://www.newyorker.com/magazine/2017/02/06/inside-the-trial-of-dylann-roof.

2. Ben Witherington, *Matthew*, Smith and Helwys Bible Commentary (Macon, GA: Smith and Helwys, 2006), 139.

3. However, the word *atonement* (at-one-ment) that Tyndale invented is better translated throughout the Old Testament as *reconciliation* (see the Common English Bible).

4. Richard Hays, "The Word of Reconciliation," *Faith and Leadership*, July 19, 2010, www.faithandleadership.com/word-reconciliation.

8. The Local Option

1. Yuval Levin, *The Fractured Republic: Renewing America's Social Contract in the Age of Individualism* (New York: Basic, 2016), 183.

2. Ibid., 165.

3. Richard B. Hays, *First Corinthians*, Interpretation (Louisville: John Knox, 1997), 220–21.

4. The Arbinger Institute, *The Anatomy of Peace: Resolving the Heart of Conflict, 2nd ed.* (Oakland, CA: Berrett-Koehler, 2015).

9. Just Resolution

1. Stanley Hauerwas, *Matthew*, Brazos Theological Commentary on the Bible (Grand Rapids: Brazos, 2015; repr., 2006), 35.

2. *The Anatomy of Peace*, 52.

3. See Lesslie Newbigin's masterful commentary *The Light Has Come: An Exposition of the Fourth Gospel* (Grand Rapids: Eerdmans, 1987).

4. Howard Zehr, *The Little Book of Restorative Justice*, rev. ed. (Brattleboro, VT: Good Books, 2015).

5. Ephraim Radner and Philip Turner, *The Fate of Communion: The Agony of Anglicanism and the Future of a Global Church* (Grand Rapids: Eerdmans, 2007), 199–200.

6. Parker Palmer, "On Staying at the Table" (unpublished manuscript).

7. *The Anatomy of Peace*, 80.

8. Ibid.

10. Bridges

1. Rowan Williams, *Being Christian* (Grand Rapids: Eerdmans, 2014), 14–15.

2. Lesslie Newbigin, *The Light Has Come: An Exposition of the Fourth Gospel* (Grand Rapids: Eerdmans, 1987), 223.

3. Karl Barth, *Church Dogmatics*, III/2:216.

4. *Donald Miller, Building a StoryBrand: Clarify Your Message So Customers Will Listen* (New York: HarperCollins Leadership, 2017).

4. Chimamanda Ngozi Adichie, "The Danger of a Single Story," TED, July 2009, https://www.ted.com/talks/chimamanda_adichie_the_danger_of_a_single_story?language=en.

5. This is a prayer authored by one of my mentors and teachers, Thomas Langford.

Afterword

1. L. Gregory Jones, *Christian Social Innovation: Renewing Wesleyan Witness* (Nashville: Abingdon, 2016).

2. See her *Christian Mission* (West Sussex: Wiley-Blackwell, 2009), 11. I am grateful to Grant Hagiya for his essay "Engage for the Benefit of the World" in *Missio Dei and the United States* (Nashville: GBHEM, 2018), and his reference to Dana Robert's work.